مؤمن للنخلة

REFLECTIONS

OF THE BELIEVER'S RESEMBLANCE TO

THE DATE TREE

SHAYKH 'ABDUR RAZZAAQ BIN ABDIL-MUHSIN AL-'ABBAD AL-BADR

First Edition, February 2013/Rabee' Thani 1434 H

Cover Design By: www.strictlysunnahdesigns.com

Translation by Ihsân Ibn Gerald Gonsalves

Revision of Translation by Abu Sulaymaan Muhammad 'Abdul-Azim Ibn Baker

Formatting and typesetting by Aboo Sulaymaan Muhammad 'Abdul Azim bin Joshua Baker

Website: www.maktabatulirshad.com

Email: info@maktabatulirshad.com

Subject: Usūl-ul-Deen

مكتبة الإرشاد
Maktabatul-Irshad
PUBLICATIONS

فهرس

TABLE OF CONTENTS

BRIEF BIOGRAPHY OF THE AUTHOR

His name: Shaykh 'Abdur Razzaaq Bin 'Abdil-Muhsin al-'Abbad al-Badr.
He is the son of Al-'Allamah Muhaddith of Medina Shaykh 'Abdul-Muhsin Al-'Abbad Al-Badr.

Birth: He was born on the 22nd day of Dhul-Qaddah in the year 1382 AH in az-Zal'fi, Kingdom of Saudia Arabia. He currently resides in Al-Medina Al-Munawwarah.

Current occupation: He is a member of the teaching staff in the Islamic University, in Al-Medina.

Scholastic certifications: Doctorate in 'Aqeedah.

The Shaykh has authored books, researches, as well as numerous explanations in different sciences. Among them:

1. Fiqh of Supplications & Ad-Dhkaar.

2. Hajj & refinement of Souls,

4

3. Explanation of the book "Exemplary Principles" By Shaykh 'Uthaymeen رحمه الله (May Allâh have mercy upon him).

4. Explanation of the book "the principles of Names & Attributes" authored by Shaykh-ul-Islam Ibn Qayyum (May Allâh have mercy upon him).

5. Explanation of the book "Good Words" authored by Shaykh-ul-Islam Ibn Qayyim (May Allâh have mercy upon him).

6. Explanation of the book "Aqeedah Tahaawiyyah".

7. Explanation of the book "Fusuul: Biography of the Messenger) By Ibn Katheer (May Allâh have mercy upon him).

8. He has a full explanation of the book "Aadaab-ul-Muf'rad" authored by Imam Bukhari (May Allâh have mercy upon him).

From the most distinguished scholars whom he has taken knowledge and acquired knowledge from are:

5

1. His father Al-'Allamah Shaykh 'Abdul-Muhsin Al-Badr—may Allâh preserve him.

2. Al-'Allamah Shaykh Ibn Baaz—may Allâh have mercy upon him.

3. Al-'Allamah Shaykh Muhammad Bin Saleh Al-'Uthaymeen—may Allâh have mercy upon him.

4. Shaykh 'Ali Nasir Faqeehi—may Allâh preserve him.

REFLECTIONS OF THE BELIEVER'S RESEMBLANCE TO THE DATE TREE

INTRODUCTION

بِـسْـمِ اللهِ الـرَّحْـمَـنِ الـرَّحِـيـمِ

All praise is for Allâh, who planted the tree of belief in the hearts of those He chooses for His servitude; and specified for his abundant excellence and blessings and those He preferred for His beneficence and mercy over the rest of His creation. So it is...

﴿ كَشَجَرَةٍ طَيِّبَةٍ أَصْلُهَا ثَابِتٌ وَفَرْعُهَا فِى ٱلسَّمَآءِ ٢٤ تُؤْتِى أُكُلَهَا كُلَّ حِينٍ بِإِذْنِ رَبِّهَا ﴾

"Like a goodly word as a goodly tree, whose root is firmly fixed, and its branches (reach) to the sky (i.e. Very high). Giving its fruit at all times, by the Leave of its Lord." [1]

May peace and blessings be upon our prophet, Muhammad, the servant of Allâh, His

---

[1] Ibrahim [14:24-25]

7

messenger, the best of His creation, the one entrusted with His revelation, His ambassador between Himself and His servants. He sent Him as a mercy to His creation, an example for mankind and a way to be followed. May Allâh bless his family and companions. As for what comes next:

It cannot escape any of the Muslims the enormous importance of *Eemaan* and its lofty, high ranking status and a high, superior level. It is the greatest of demands, a magnificent intention, and a noble goal; since, by it, the servant obtains happiness in this life and the next. With it, the servant knows the most crucial things to seek and the noblest goals. By it, the servant gains heaven and its pleasures. By it, the servant will be saved from the hellfire and the displeasure of The Almighty. By it, the servant earns the pleasure of our Lord and never displeases him. By it, he delights in looking at the face of The Most Noble without any adversity or trial. The fruits of *Eemaan* and its benefits are too many to count. How many great benefits, ripe fruit, and continuing good in this life and the next do *Eemaan* possess!?

Since *Eemaan* is this equivalent and this worth of importance, then the texts which clarify its virtue and shows the distinction of its value are immensely abundant and various. Since verily from Allâh's complete wisdom and abundant blessings upon his servants is that He made the matter so that whenever the need for something is great and necessary and the want more dire, then the proofs for it and ways to achieve it are amply provided and more abundant.

The servant's need for *Eemaan* is the greatest of needs. It is greater than their need for food or drink and the rest of their affairs. So because of that, the proofs for *Eemaan* are the strongest of evidences, its proofs are the most authentic proofs, and the pathways towards attaining and gaining it are the easiest of paths to tread (upon), the nearest of it (the paths) to adopt, and the most facilitated of it (the paths) to reach.

So for that reason, the proofs for *Eemaan* are numerous and varied, and its evidences that clarify it (*Eemaan*) in a general and specific sense.

INTRODUCTION

Verily some of the greatest proofs for *Eemaan* that the Quran consists are those verses that contain parables that clarify the reality of *Eemaan* and make clear its details and branches and its fruit and its benefits become apparent.

A parable is a statement that compares one thing to another due to a resemblance between them in order to clarify one from the other and to form it in the mind, and there is no doubt that using parables and examples improve understanding. It does so by bringing to the mind something tangible. Allah says (and His speech consists of the greatest, most definitive proofs):

﴿ وَتِلْكَ ٱلْأَمْثَٰلُ نَضْرِبُهَا لِلنَّاسِ وَمَا يَعْقِلُهَآ إِلَّا ٱلْعَٰلِمُونَ ۝ ﴾

"And these similitudes we put forward for mankind, but none will understand them except those who have knowledge (of Allâh and His Signs, etc.)." [2]

---

[2] Al-Ankabut [29:43]

The Quran contains over forty parables, and some of the Salaf, whenever they would read a parable from the Quran that they did not understand they would burst into tears and say:

"I am not from the knowledgeable people". [3]

Qatada used to say:

اِعْقِلُوا عَنِ اللهِ الْأَمْثَالَ

"Understand Allâh through the parables". [4]

I thought that I would present this lesson on one of the similitudes from the Quran and the *Sunnah* that includes a clarification of *Eemaan*, its approximation, and an elucidation of its origin, its branches and its fruit, due to this (i.e.

---

[3] From the book: *"Al-Kaafiyah Ash-Shaafiyah"* by Ibnul-Qayyim (page 9).

[4] Abi Hatim noted it just as what is in the book: *"Ad-Durr Al-Man'thur"* by As-Suyuuti (5/26)

INTRODUCTION

The previous mentioned verse), and from Allâh alone is the success and help.

THE PARABLE OF THE GOODLY TREE

Allâh ﷻ says:

﴿ أَلَمْ تَرَ كَيْفَ ضَرَبَ ٱللَّهُ مَثَلًا كَلِمَةً طَيِّبَةً كَشَجَرَةٍ طَيِّبَةٍ أَصْلُهَا ثَابِتٌ وَفَرْعُهَا فِى ٱلسَّمَآءِ ۝ تُؤْتِى أُكُلَهَا كُلَّ حِينٍ بِإِذْنِ رَبِّهَا وَيَضْرِبُ ٱللَّهُ ٱلْأَمْثَالَ لِلنَّاسِ لَعَلَّهُمْ يَتَذَكَّرُونَ ۝ ﴾

"See you not how Allâh sets forth a parable? - A goodly word as a goodly tree, whose root is firmly fixed, and its branches (reach) to the sky (i.e. Very high). Giving its fruit at all times, by the Leave of its Lord and Allâh sets forth parables for mankind in order that they may remember." [5]

This is a remarkable parable with an enormous benefit and applies perfectly to that which it is being compared with. Allâh begins the verse by saying,

---

[5] Ibrahim [14:24-25]

أَلَمۡ تَرَ كَيۡفَ ضَرَبَ ٱللَّهُ مَثَلًا

"See you not how Allâh sets forth a parable?"[6]

Meaning, does not your heart see and comprehend how Allâh makes an example and a comparison for the *"goodly word"*, the word of *Eemaan*. Allâh finishes the verse with:

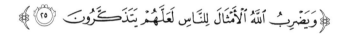

"Allâh sets forth parables for mankind in order that they may remember." [7]

Meaning: that the intention behind this parable and others, are to remind the people and invite them to consider and understand the speech of Allâh.

There can be no doubt that this beginning and end to the verse are the best of encouragements

---

6 Ibrahim [14:24]

7 Ibrahim [14:25]

for a person to learn and understand this parable. They also show the enormous importance of this parable and how it includes *Eemaan*, which is the best thing for a person to seek and the greatest goal. When we consider this splendid parable we find that Allâh mentions the thing that is being compared, the thing it is being compared to and the similarity between them. The thing that is being compared is *"the good word"*, the thing it is being compared to is *"the tree"*, and the similarity between them is like Allâh says:

$$ \text{﴿أَصْلُهَا ثَابِتٌ وَفَرْعُهَا فِى ٱلسَّمَآءِ ۝ تُؤْتِى أُكُلَهَا كُلَّ حِينٍ بِإِذْنِ رَبِّهَا﴾} $$

"Whose root is firmly fixed, and its branches (reach) to the sky (i.e. Very high); giving its fruit at all times, by the Leave of its Lord." [8]

Allâh, The Blessed, The Most High, compares the *Eemaan* that is firm in the heart of the believer and that which results from that *Eemaan* in the

---

[8] Ibrahim [14:24]

15

way of branches, divisions and fruit, with the "goodly tree" whose roots are firm, its branches outstretched into the sky, and always produces fruit.

So if, one was to consider the thing being compared to, which is the tree, and the thing being compared, which is the proclamation of *Eemaan* that is in the heart of the believer and that which results from it, then they will find that they share many similar characteristics, some of which are mentioned in the verse. Ibn Al-Qayyim رحمه الله (may Allâh have mercy upon him) said:

إِذَا تَأَمَّلْتَ هَذَا التَّشْبِيهَ رَأَيْتَهُ مُطَابِقاً لِشَجَرَةِ التَّوْحِيدِ الثَّابِتَةِ الرَّاسِخَةِ فِي الْقَلْبِ، الَّتِي فُرُوعُهَا مِنَ الْأَعْمَالِ الصَّالِحَةِ صَاعِدَةً إِلَى السَّمَاءِ، وَ لَا تَزَالُ هَذِهِ الشَّجَرَةُ تُثْمِرُ الْأَعْمَالَ الصَّالِحَةَ كُلَّ وَقْتٍ، بِحَسَبِ ثَبَاتِهَا فِي الْقَلْبِ، وَ مَحَبَّةِ الْقَلْبِ لَهَا، وَ إِخْلَاصِهِ فِيهَا، وَ مَعْرِفَتِهِ بِحَقِيقَتِهَا، وَ قِيَامِهِ بِحُقُوقِهَا، وَ مُرَاعَاتِهَا حَقَّ رَعَايَتِهَا، فَمَنْ

رَسَخَتْ هَذِهِ الْكَلِمَةُ فِي قَلْبِهِ بِحَقِيقَتِهَا الَّتِي هِيَ
حَقِيقَتُهَا ، وَاتَّصَفَ قَلْبُهُ بِهَا ، وَانْصَبَغَ بِهَا
بِصِبْغَةِ اللهِ الَّتِي لَا أَحْسَنَ صِبْغَةً مِـ
نْهَا ، فَعَرَفَ حَقِيقَةَ الْإِلَهِيَّةِ الَّتِي يُثْبِتُهَا قَلْبُهُ لله وَ
يَشْهَدُ بِهَا لِسَانُهُ وَ تُصَدِّقُهَا جَوَارِحُهُ ، وَ نَفَى تِلْكَ
الْحَقِيقَةَ وَ لَوَازِمَهَا عَنْ كُلِّ مَا سِوَى اللهِ ، وَ وَاطَأَ
قَلْبُهُ لِسَانَهُ فِي هَذَا النَّفِي وَالْإِثْبَاتِ ، وَانْقَادَتْ
جَوَارِجُهُ لِمَنْ شَهِدَ لَهُ بِالْوَحْدَانِيَّةِ طَائِعَةً سَالِكَةً
سُبُلَ رَبِّهِ ذُلُلاً غَيْرَ نَاكِبَةٍ عَنْهَا وَ لَا بَاغِيَةَ سَوَاهَا
بَدَلاً ، كَمَا لَا يَبْتَغِي الْقَلْبُ سِوَى مَعْبُودِهِ الْحَقِّ
بَدَلاً ، فَلَا رَيْبَ أَنَّ هَذِهِ الْكَلِمَةَ مِنْ هَذَا الْقَلْبِ عَلَى
هَذَا اللِّسَانِ لَا تَزَالُ تُؤْتِي ثَمَرَتَهَا مِنَ الْعَمَلِ الصَّالِحِ
الصَّاعِدِ إِلَى اللهِ كُلَّ وَقْتٍ، فَهَذِهِ الْكَلِمَةُ الطَّيِّبَةُ هِيَ
الَّتِي رَفَعَتْ هَذَا الْعَمَلَ الصَّالِحَ إِلَى الرَّبِّ تَعَالَى ، وَ
هَذِهِ الْكَلِمَةُ الطَّيِّبَةُ تُثْمِرُ كَلِماً كَثِيراً طَيِّباً

17

يُقَارِنُهُ عَمَلٌ صَالِحٌ فَيَرْفَعُ الْعَمَلُ الصَّالِحُ الْكَلِمَ الطَّيِّبَ ، كَمَا قَالَ تَعَالَى : ﴿إِلَيْهِ يَصْعَدُ ٱلْكَلِمُ ٱلطَّيِّبُ وَٱلْعَمَلُ ٱلصَّلِحُ يَرْفَعُهُۥۚ﴾ فَأَخْبَرَ سُبْحَانَهُ أَنَّ الْعَمَلَ الصَّالِحَ يَرْفَعُ الْكَلِمَ الطَّيِّبَ ، وَ أَخْبَرَ أَنَّ الْكَلِمَةَ الطَّيِّبَةَ تُثْمِرُ لِقَائِلِهَا عَمَلاً صَالِحاً كُلَّ وَقْتٍ . وَ الْمَقْصُودُ أَنَّ كَلِمَةَ التَّوْحِيدِ إِذَا شَهِدَ بِهَا الْمُؤْمِنُ عَارِفاً بِمَعْنَاهَا وَ حَقِيقَتِهَا نَفِياً وَ إِثْبَاتاً ، مُتَّصِفاً بِمُوجِبِهَا قَائِماً قَلْبُهُ وَ لِسَانُهُ وَ جَوَارِجُهُ بِشَهَادَتِهِ ، فَهَذِهِ الْكَلِمَةُ الطَّيِّبَةُ هِيَ الَّتِي رَفَعَتْ هَذَا الْعَمَلَ مِنْ هَذَا الشَّاهِدِ ، أَصْلُهَا ثَابَتْ ، رَاسِخٌ فِي قَلْبِهِ ، وَ فُرُوعُهَا مُتَّصِلَةٌ بِالسَّمَاءِ ، وَ هِيَ مُخْرِجَةٌ لِثَمَرَتِهَا كُلَّ وَقْتٍ .

"If you were to consider this resemblance you would see that it applies to the tree of Tawheed that is firmly rooted in the heart; its branches are the righteous actions which reach high into the sky and this tree never

18

stops producing good deeds. The amount of righteous actions is dependent upon the extent that Tawheed is embedded in the heart, the extent of the love the heart has for Tawheed, the extent of sincerity one has for Tawheed, the extent of knowledge one has of Tawheed, the extent one applies Tawheed, the extent one performs its rights, and the extent that one takes care of it.

Whoever firmly roots the proclamation of Eemaan in their heart and characterizes their heart by it and anoints it with the religion of Allâh, of which there is no better religion, and then he knows the reality of divinity, which his heart affirms for Allâh alone and he bears witness to that with his tongue and confirms that with his limbs. He negates this divinity and that which it necessitates, for everything other than for Allâh; and his heart agrees with the tongue in this negation and affirmation and his limbs submit to that which he testifies to with Tawheed, obediently walking the path of his Lord with humility, without deviation and without desiring another to replace it.

There's no doubt that this proclamation in the heart and on the tongue continually produces good deeds that raise up to Allâh all the time. This goodly word is what raises up the righteous actions to Allah and produces many goodly words hand in hand with righteous actions. Allâh, the Most High, says:

"To Him ascend (all) the goodly words and the righteous deeds exalt it (the goodly words i.e. The goodly words are not accepted by Allâh unless and until they are followed by good deeds)"

So he informs us that the righteous deeds raise up "the goodly words" and He informs us that the "goodly words" produce righteous deeds all the time. What is meant is if the believer bears witness to the testification of Tawheed, knowing its meaning and the reality of it in regards to its negation and affirmation and distinguishes himself with the characteristics of Tawheed and makes his heart, tongue and limbs upright with this testification, then it is this goodly word that raises up the good deeds from the person who testifies to it. Its roots are firm in his heart, and its branches reach into the sky, and it gives out fruit all the time.

Therefore, it is this goodly word that raises the actions from this witness. Its root is firmly rooted in his heart; its branches reach into the sky, and produces its fruit constantly." [9]

It is authentically narrated from the Prophet that *"the goodly tree"* is the date tree. What is narrated by Ibn Umar (may Allâh be pleased with him) and reported in Bukhari and Muslim via numerous chains of narration. Al-Bukhari and Muslim narrated from Isma'il bin Ja'far, who narrated from Abdullah bin Dinar, who narrated from Ibn Umar that he said: "The Messenger of Allâh (may peace and blessings be upon him) said:

إِنَّ مِنَ الـشَّـجَرِ شَـجَرَةً لَا يَسْـقُطُ وَرَقُهَا ، وَ إِنَّهَا مِثْلُ الْـمُسْـلِمِ ، فَحَدِّثُونِي مَا هِيَ ؟ فَوَقَعَ النَّـاسُ فِي شَـجَرِ

الْبَوَادِي . قَالَ عَبْدُ الله : وَ وَقَعَ فِي نَفْسِي أَنَّهَا
النَّخْلَةُ ، فَاسْتَحْيَيْتُ ، ثُمَّ قَالُوا: حَدِّثْنَا مَا هِيَ يَا
رَسُولَ الله ؟ فَقَالَ : هِيَ النَّخْلَةُ . قَالَ : فَذَكَرْتُ ذَلِكَ
لِعُمَرَ . قَالَ : لِأَنْ تَكُونَ قُلْتَ : هِيَ النَّخْلَةُ ، أَحَبُّ
إِلَيَّ مِنْ كَذَا وَ كَذَا .

"Verily there is a tree whose leaves do not fall and it resembles the Muslim. Tell me what it is?' The people thought that it was one of the desert trees." Abdullah ibn Umar said: "I thought that it was the date tree, but I felt shy. Then the people said: 'Tell us what it is O Messenger of Allâh', so he said: 'It is the Date tree.' I told Umar and he said: 'If you had said it is the date tree that would be more loved to me such and such." [10]

This wording is from Muslim. Al-Bukhari also reported it by way of Sulaymaan who narrated it from Abdullah bin Dinar and by way of Malik who also narrated it from Abdullah bin Dinar.

---

[10] Al-Bukhari (1/38), and Muslim (4/2164)

22

Bukhari and Muslim narrated from Ibn Abi
Nujayh, who narrated that Mujahid said:

صَحِبْتُ ابْنَ عُمَرَ إِلَى الْمَدِينَةِ فَلَمْ أَسْمَعْهُ يُحَدِّثُ

عَنْ رَسُولِ الله - صلَّى اللهُ عَلَيْهِ وَ سَلَّمَ - إِلَّا حَدِيثًا

وَاحِدًا قَالَ : كُنَّا عِنْدَ النَّبِيِّ - صَلَّى اللهُ عَلَيْهِ وَ

سَلَّمَ ، فَأُتِيَ بِجُمَّارٍ ، فَقَالَ : ((إِنَّ مِنَ الشَّجَرِ

شَجَرَةً مِثْلُهَا كَمَثَلِ الْمُسْلِمِ)) . فَأَرَدْتُ أَنْ أَقُولَ هِيَ

النَّخْلَةُ ، فَإِذَا أَنَا أَصْغَرُ الْقَوْمِ فَسَكَتُّ . قَالَ النَّبِيُّ -

صَلَّى اللهُ عَلَيْهِ وَ سَلَّم - : ((هِيَ النَّخْلَةُ)) .

'I accompanied Ibn Umar to Medina, and he
did not speak about the Messenger of Allâh
(may peace and blessings be upon him)
except for one hadith, he said: "We were with
the Prophet, and a date tree heart was
brought to him, so he said: 'There is a tree its
example is like the example of a Muslim' I
wanted to say it is the date tree, but I was
the youngest of the group, so I did not say
anything. The Prophet (may peace and

blessings be upon him) said: 'It is the Date Tree." [11]

Bukhari reported by way of Abi Bashr, who narrated from Mujahid, who narrated from Ibn Umar (may Allâh be pleased with him) that he said:

كُنْتُ عِنْدَ النَّبِيِّ - صَلَّى اللهُ عَلَيْهِ وَ سَلَّمَ - وَ هُوَ يَأْكُلُ جُمَّاراً ، فَقَالَ : ((مِنَ الشَّجَرِ شَجَرَةٌ كَالرَّجُلِ الْمُؤْمِنِ)) فَأَرَدْتُ أَنْ أَقُولَ هِيَ النَّخْلَةُ ، فَإِذَا أَنَا أَحْدَثُهُمْ . قَالَ : ((هِيَ النَّخْلَةُ)) .

"I was with the Prophet (may peace and blessings be upon him), and he was eating a date tree heart, and he said, 'There is a tree that resembles a believing man." So I wanted to say it is the date tree, but I was the youngest of them. Then he said, 'It's the date tree'." [12]

---

[11] Al-Bukhari (1/43), and Muslim (4/2165)

[12] Al-Bukhari (2/115)

Bukhari reported via Al-A'mash He said, "Mujahid narrated to me who narrated from Abdullah ibn Umar (may Allâh be pleased with him) that he said:

بَيْنَمَا نَحْنُ عِنْدَ النَّبِيِّ - صَلَّى اللهُ عَلَيْهِ وَ سَلَّمَ - جُلُوسٌ ، إِذْ أُتِيَ بِجُمَّارِ نَخْلَةٍ ، فَقَالَ النَّبِيُّ - صَلَّى اللهُ عَلَيْهِ وَ سَلَّمَ - : إِنَّ مِنَ الشَّجَرِ لَمَا بَرَكَتُهُ كَبَرَكَةِ الْمُسْلِمِ)) . فَظَنَنْتُ أَنَّهُ يَعْنِي النَّخْلَةَ ، فَأَرَدْتُ أَنْ أَقُولَ هِيَ النَّخْلَةُ يَا رَسُولَ اللهِ ، ثُمَّ الْتَفَتُّ فَإِذَا أَنَا عَاشِرُ عَشَرَةٍ ، أَنَا أَحْدَثُهُمْ ، فَسَكَتُّ ، فَقَالَ النَّبِيُّ - صَلَّى اللهُ عَلَيْهِ وَ سَلَّمَ: ((هِيَ النَّخْلَةُ)) .

"We were sitting with the Prophet ﷺ (may peace and blessings be upon him), and someone brought a date tree heart, then the Prophet (may peace and blessings be upon him) said: "There is a tree; its blessing is like the blessing of a believer". I thought that he meant the date tree. I wanted to say: it is the date tree O Messenger of Allâh. I looked

around and saw that out of a group of ten I was the youngest, so I did not say anything; then the Prophet (may peace and blessings be upon him) said: 'It is the Date Tree.'" [13]

Bukhari reported via Zubaid, who narrated a summary of the hadith from Mujahid. [14]

Muslim reported via Abu Khalil Ad-Duba'i, who narrated from Mujahid, who narrated from Ibn Umar that the Prophet (may peace and blessings be upon him) said one day to his companions:

((أَخْبِرُونِي عَنْ شَجَرَةٍ، مِثْلُهَا مِثْلُ الْمُؤْمِنِ))، فَجَعَلَ الْقَوْمُ يَذْكُرُونَ شَجَراً مِنَ الْبَوَادِي. قَالَ ابْنُ عُمَرَ: وَ أُلْقِيَ فِي نَفْسِي أَوْ روعي أَنَّهَا النَّخْلَةُ. فَجَعَلْتُ أُرِيدُ أَنْ أَقُولَهَا، فَإِذَا أَسْنَانُ الْقَوْمِ، فَأَهَابُ أَنْ أَتَكَلَّمَ، فَلَمَّا سَكَتُوا، قَالَ رَسُولُ اللهِ - صَلَّى اللهُ عَلَيْهِ وَ سَلَّمَ : ((هِيَ النَّخْلَةُ)).

"Tell me about a tree that resembles the believer", so the people began to mention a tree from the desert. Ibn Umar said: "It occurred to me that it was the date tree. I wanted to say it, but I found the elders of the people were present, so I was scared to talk. When they did not say anything the Messenger of Allâh (may peace and blessings be upon him) said: "It's the date tree." [15]

Muslim also reported the hadith via Saif, who narrated it from Mujahid. [16]

Bukhari and Muslim narrated from Ubaidullah bin Umar, who narrated from Nafi', who narrated from Ibn Umar (may Allâh have mercy upon him) he said:

كُنَّا عِنْدَ رَسُولِ الله ‎- صَلَّى اللهُ عَلَيْهِ وَ سَلَّمَ - فَقَالَ :
أَخْبِرُونِي بِشَجَرَةٍ تُشَبِّهُ أَوْ كَالرَّجُلِ الْمُسْلِمِ لَا
يَتَحَاتُّ وَرَقُهَا وَ لَا وَ لَا وَ لَا ، تُؤْتِي أُكُلُهَا كُلَّ حِينٍ .

---

15 Muslim (4/2165)
16 Muslim (4/2166)

27

قَالَ ابْنُ عُمَرَ : فَوَقَعَ فِي نَفْسِي أَنَّهَا النَّخْلَةُ ، وَ
رَأَيْتُ أَبَا بَكْرٍ وَ عُمَرَ لَا يَتَكَلَّمَانِ ، فَكَرِهْتُ أَنْ
أَتَكَلَّمَ ، فَلَمَّا لَمْ يَقُولُواْ شَيْئاً قَالَ رَسُولُ الله – صَلَّى
اللهُ عَلَيْهِ وَ سَلَّمَ : هِيَ النَّخْلَةُ . فَلَمَّا قُمْنَا قُلْتُ
لِعُمَرَ : يَا أَبَتَاهُ ، وَ الله لَقَدْ وَقَعَ فِي نَفْسِي أَنَّهَا
النَّخْلَةُ ، فَقَالَ : مَا مَنَعَكَ أَنْ تَكَلَّمَ ؟ قَالَ : لَمْ
أَرَكُم تَكَلَّمُونَ فَكَرِهْتُ أَنْ أَتَكَلَّمَ أَوْ أَقُولَ شَيْئاً . قَالَ
عُمْرَ : لَأَنْ تَكُونُ قُلْتَهَا أَحَبُّ إِلَيَّ مِنْ كَذَا وَ كَذَا)) .

"We were with the Messenger of Allâh (May peace and blessings be upon him) who said: 'Tell me of a tree that resembles the Muslim man. Its leaves do not fall; it does not..., It does not..., It does not.... It brings sustenance all the time'" Ibn Umar said: "It occurred to me that it was the date tree, but I saw Abu Bakr and Umar did not say anything, so I did not want to speak. When they did not say anything, the Messenger of Allâh said: 'It is the date tree'" After the people rose to leave, I said to Umar: "O

28

Father by Allah I thought it was the date
tree", so he said: 'What stopped you from
saying that?' He said: "I saw that no one
spoke, so I did not want to say anything".
Umar said: "If you had spoken it would have
been more beloved to me than so and so". [17]

Bukhari reported via Maharib bin Dithar, who
heard Ibn Umar say:

قَالَ النَّبِيُّ - صَلَّى اللهُ عَلَيْهِ وَ سَلَّمَ -: ((مَثَلُ الْمُؤْمِنِ
كَمَثَلِ شَجَرَةٍ خَضْرَاءَ ، لَا يَسْقُطُ وَرَقُهَا وَ لَا يَتَحَاتُّ
. فَقَالَ الْقَوْمُ : هِيَ النَّخْلَةُ - وَ أَنَا غُلَامٌ شَابٌّ -
فَاسْتَحْيَيْتُ ، فَقَالَ : هِيَ النَّخْلَةُ)) .

"The Prophet (may peace and blessings be
upon him) said: 'The Muslim is like a green
tree whose leaves do not fall.' The people
said: 'Its tree so and so or tree so and so'. I
wanted to say that it was the date tree, but I
was a young boy, so I was shy to speak. The

17 Al-Bukhari (3/246) and Muslim (4/2166)

Prophet (may peace and blessings be upon him) said: 'It's the date tree'" [18]

Bukhari reported via Hafs bin Asim, who narrated from Ibn Umar something similar. [19]

This is everything that was reported in Bukhari and Muslim, in regards to this great hadith from the different chains of narration. There are also other chains reported in other than Bukhari and Muslim in the various *sunnan*, *masanid*, and *ma'ajim*, as will be seen in that which follows.

Bukhari, May Allâh have mercy upon him, mentioned this hadith in a number of different places in his *Saheeh*. He reported it in *"The Book of Tafsir"* in the section named after the verse:

$$﴿ كَشَجَرَةٍ طَيِّبَةٍ أَصْلُهَا ثَابِتٌ وَفَرْعُهَا فِي ٱلسَّمَاءِ ۝ تُؤْتِىٓ أُكُلَهَا كُلَّ حِينٍ ﴾$$

---

[18] Saheeh-ul-Bukhari (4/113)
[19] Saheeh-ul-Bukhari (4/113)

"As a goodly tree, whose root is firmly fixed, and its branches (reach) to the sky (i.e. Very high). Giving its fruit at all times." [20]

He indicates that the tree mentioned in the verse is the date tree, so the hadith, therefore, explains the verse.

This is mentioned clearly in the hadith reported by Al-Bazzar via Moosa bin Uqbah, who narrated from Nafi', who narrated from Ibn Umar who said that the Messenger of Allâh read the verse:

$$﴿ أَلَمْ تَرَ كَيْفَ ضَرَبَ ٱللَّهُ مَثَلًا كَلِمَةً طَيِّبَةً كَشَجَرَةٍ طَيِّبَةٍ ﴾$$

"See you not how Allâh sets forth a parable? - A goodly word as a goodly tree."

Then he said:

أَتَدْرُونَ مَا هِيَ؟ قَالَ ابْنُ عُمَرَ: لَمْ يَخْفَ عَلَيَّ أَنَّهَا النَّخْلَةُ، فَمَنَعَنِي أَنْ أَتَكَلَّمَ مَكَانَ سِنِّي، فَقَالَ رَسُولُ اللهِ – صَلَّى اللهُ عَلَيْهِ وَ سَلَّمَ: هِيَ النَّخْلَةُ)).

"Do you know what it is?" Ibn Umar said: "It was apparent to me that it was the date tree, but my young age prevented me from speaking". The Prophet then said: "It is the date tree" 21

Ibn Hajar said:

وَ يُجْمَعُ بَيْنَ هَذَا وَ بَيْنَ مَا تَقَدَّمَ أَنَّهُ – صَلَّى اللهُ عَلَيْهِ وَ سَلَّمَ – أُتِيَ بِالْجُمَّارِ فَشَرَعَ فِي أَكْلِهِ تَالِياً لِلْآيَةِ قَائِلاً: إِنَّ مِنَ الشَّجَرِ شَجَرَةً ... إِلَى آخِرِهِ.

"Combining between this hadith and that which was mentioned previously: he (may peace and blessings be upon him) was brought a date tree heart and he began to eat

---

21 Al-Hafidh mentioned it in his explanation of Saheeh Bukhari: *"Fath-ul-Baari"* (1/146)

**it after having read the verse, and he said:
"There is a tree..." To the end of the hadith.**

Ibn Hiban reported the narration of Abdul Aziz
bin Muslim, who narrated from Abdullah bin
Dinar, who narrated from Ibn Umar that Prophet
ﷺ (may peace and blessings be upon him)
said:

((مَنْ يُخْبِرُنِي عَنْ شَجَرَةٍ مِثْلُهَا مِثْلُ الْمُؤْمِنِ،
أَصْلُهَا ثَابِتٌ وَ فَرْعُهَا فِي السَّمَاء ؟ ....))

**"Who can tell me about a tree that resembles
the believer; its roots are firm and its
branches are in the sky...?"** [22]

This strengthens Al-Bazzar's narration. What
also strengthens this are the many narrations
from the companions and others that explained
the *"goodly tree"* as the date tree.

At-Tirmidhi and others reported from Shuaib bin
Al-Habhaab who said:

---

[22] Fath-ul-Baari (1 / 146,147)

كُنَّا عِنْدَ أَنَسٍ فَأَتَيْنَا بِطَبَقٍ عَلَيْهِ رَطَبٌ ، فَقَالَ أَنَسٌ
- رَضِيَ اللهُ عَنْهُ - لِأَبِي الْعَالِيَةِ : ((كُلْ يَا أَبَا الْعَالِيَةِ ،
فَإِنَّ هَذَا مِنَ الشَّجَرَةِ الَّتِي ذَكَرَ اللهُ فِي كِتَابِهِ ﴿ضَرَبَ
اللَّهُ مَثَلًا كَلِمَةً طَيِّبَةً كَشَجَرَةٍ طَيِّبَةٍ أَصْلُهَا ثَابِتٌ ﴾ قَالَ : هَكَذَا
قَرَأَهَا يَوْمَئِذٍ أَنَسٌ)).

**"We were with Anas, and he brought us a
plate of dates, then he (may Allâh be pleased
with him) said to Abu Aliyah: 'Eat Abu Aliyah
for verily this is from the tree that Allâh
mentioned in his book: 'Allâh sets forth a
parable? - A goodly word as a goodly tree,
whose root is firmly fixed'. He said: 'This is
how Anas read it,"** 23

At-Tirmidhi also narrated similar to this but
attributed it to the Prophet (may peace and
blessings be upon him). He said:

---

23 Sunan At-Tirmidhi (#3119), and 'Abd-ur-Razzaaq, Ibn Jarir,
Ibn Al-Munthir, Ibn Abi Hatim, and Al-Ramharam'zee in the
book "the parables" just like what is in the book *"Ad-Durr Al-
Man'thur"* authored by As-Suutiyii (5/22)

هَـذَا الْـمَـوْقُـوفُ أَصَـحُّ .

"It's more authentic that this hadith was not said by the Prophet (May peace and blessings be upon him)".

Ibn Abbas, Mujahid, Masrooq, Ikramah, Ad-Dahaak, Qatadah, Ibn Zaid, and others gave the same explanation for this verse.

The Prophet (may peace and blessings be upon him) expressed this aforementioned explanation, i.e. The resemblance of the believer to the date tree, in the most concise words in that which At-Tabarani reported in *Al-Mu'jam Al-Kabir* and Al-Bazzar from the hadith of Ibn Umar (may Allâh be pleases with him):

مَثَلُ الْـمُـؤْمِـنِ مَثَلُ الـنَّـخْـلَـةِ مَا أَخَـذْتَ مِـنْـهَا مِـنْ شَـيْـئٍ
نَـفَـعَـكَ

"Example of the believer is like that of the date tree: whatever you take from it benefits you" [24]

The date tree was given the excellence of resembling the believing servant of Allâh because it is the best of the trees and most beneficial. Abu Hatim As-Sijistani wrote a book solely for the date tree. In it, he explained its excellence, its features and its different names. In it, he considers a number of issues concerning the date tree. In the beginning he says:

النَّخْلَةُ سَيِّدَةُ الشَّجَرِ ، مَخْلُوقَةٌ مِنْ طِينِ آدَمَ صَلَوَاتُ اللهِ عَلَيْهِ ، وَ قَدْ ضَرَبَهَا اللهُ جَلَّ وَ عَزَّ مَثَلاً ((لَا إِلَهَ إِلَّا اللهُ)) فَقَالَ تَبَارَكَ وَ تَعَالَى : ﴿ أَلَمْ تَرَ كَيْفَ ضَرَبَ اللَّهُ مَثَلًا كَلِمَةً طَيِّبَةً ﴾ وَ هِيَ قَوْلُ : ((لَا إِلَهَ إِلَّا اللهُ)) ، ﴿ كَشَجَرَةٍ طَيِّبَةٍ ﴾ وَ هِيَ النَّخْلَةُ . فَكَمَا أَنَّ قَوْلَ ((لَا إِلَهَ

---

[24] the book *"Al-Mu'jam al-Kabeer"* authored by At-Tabaraanee (12/ #13514)

إِلَّا اللهُ)) سَيِّدُ الْكَلَام ، كَذَلِكَ النَّخْلَةُ سَيِّدَةُ الشَّجَرِ

. ((

"The date tree is the master of all trees; it is
created from the clay of Adam (May the
blessings of Allâh be upon him), and Allâh
made it a parable for 'la ilha illallah' (there's
none worthy of worship except Allâh), as He,
the Most Venerated, the Most High, says:
"See you not how Allâh sets forth a parable? -
A goodly word..." that is the saying: 'la ilaha
illallah' and 'as a goodly tree', and this is the
date tree.

Just as, 'la ilaha illallah' is the master of
speech, then the date tree is the master of
the trees." [25]

Then he began to speak in detail about this
noble and virtuous tree and supported his
saying that the date tree was created from the
clay of Adam (may Allâh's blessings be upon
him) with the hadith narrated via Masroor bin
Mas'ood At-Tamimi, who said:

---

25 the book *"the book of Date trees"* (page 33)

37

"Al-Awza'i told me that Urwa bin Ruwaim narrated from Ali bin Abi Talib said that the Messenger of Allâh said:

Honor your uncle, the date tree, for verily it was created from the clay that Adam was created from and it does not cross pollinate with anything else. Feed your pregnant wives with its fresh and its dried dates. There is no tree nobler with Allâh than the tree Maryam bint Imran took rest under.

The chain of narration for this hadith is not authentic so it cannot be used as a proof. This hadith was only narrated by Masroor bin Mas'ood, and he is unknown. Ibn Al-Jawzi said:

لَا يَصِحُّ عَنْ رَسُولِ اللهِ - صَلَّى اللهُ عَلَيْهِ وَ
سَلَّمَ ، قَالَ ابْنُ عُدَي : مَسْرُورٌ غَيْرُ مَعْرُوفٍ وَ
هُوَ مُنْكَرُ الْحَدِيثِ ، وَ قَالَ ابْنُ حِبَّانٍ : يَرْوِي
عَنِ الْأَوْزَاعِي الْمَنَاكِيرَ الَّتِي لَا يَجُوزُ
الْإِحْتِجَاجُ بِمَا يَرْوِيهَا . وَ قَالَ الذَّهَبِيُّ :))

غَـمَـزَهُ ابْنُ حِـبَّـانٍ ، فَـقَـالَ : يَـرْوِي عَـنِ الْأَوْزَاعِـي
الْـمَـنَـاكِـيـرَ الْكَـثِـيـرَةَ .

"This is not authentically narrated from the
Messenger of Allâh. Ibn Uday said: 'Masroor is
unknown and narrates hadith that are not
narrated by anyone else' and Ibn Hibban said:
'He narrates the weak hadith from Al-Awza'i
that is not allowed to use as a proof' [26]
And Dhahabi said: 'Ibn Hibban considered him a
weak narrator and said that he narrated a lot of
the weak hadith from Al-Awza'i'" [27]

Taking this into consideration, there is still no
doubt about the excellence of the date tree, its
nobility, and its distinction. It is enough that the
tree was singled out from the other trees as a
parable for the believer. In the previous texts, we
find a number of things that point towards some
of the date tree's many virtues and

---

26 The book: "Al-Mawduu'aat" (1/129)

27 The book: "Al-Mizaan" (5/222), and look in the book: "As-
Silsilat-ud-Dae'fah" authored by Al-'Allamah Al-Albaani, may
Allâh have mercy upon him, (1/283,284)

characteristics. For example, the strength of its roots, the height of its branches, how it produces food all the time, that every part of it is beneficial and other than that from the virtues and characteristics of the date tree.

Here, there is a pivotal point, and that is that when the Prophet ﷺ (may peace and blessings be upon him) compared the believer to the date tree it was due to numerous aspects of resemblance between the date tree and the believer. The believer that is obedient to Allâh, who has the proclamation of *Eemaan* steadfast in his heart and fills his chest, and bears ripe fruit and varied goodness.

There is no doubt about the importance of contemplating, searching for and understanding the different aspects of the resemblance between the date tree and the believer due to its great many benefits. Allâh, the Most High guides us to the understanding of these benefits when he compares the date tree and the believer and mentions a number of the characteristics shared between them, when he says:

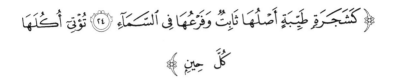

"...A goodly tree, whose root is firmly fixed, and its branches (reach) to the sky (i.e. Very high). Giving its fruit at all times..." [28]

Here are four aspects of resemblance between them, and if a person was to consider the thing being compared and the thing it is being compared to he would find many aspects of resemblance between them. Whoever reads the sayings of the people of knowledge on this subject will come upon many benefits. In the following, I hope to bring some of the aspects of resemblance that has been mentioned by the people of knowledge in the books of *Tafsir* and the various explanations of the hadith.

---

[28] Ibrahim [14:24-25]

SOME OF THE ASPECTS OF RESEMBLANCE
BETWEEN THE DATE TREE AND THE
BELIEVER

SOME OF THE ASPECTS OF RESEMBLANCE
BETWEEN THE DATE TREE AND THE BELIEVER

So among these aspects...[29]

The 1ˢᵗ aspect:

The date tree always has a trunk, branches, and fruit and likewise the tree of *Eemaan*. It must have a trunk, branches and fruit. The trunk of *Eemaan* are the well-known six foundations; its branches are the righteous deeds, the types of obedience and the many things that draw you close to Allâh; and its fruits are all the good things that happen to the believer and all the happiness that he earns in this life and the next.

Abdullah reports in the *Sunnah* narrating from *At-Tawus*, who narrated that his father said:

---

[29] Look regarding this matter in the books: *"Miftaah Dar-is-Sa'adah"* (1/116-122), *"I'laam-ul-Muwaqi'een"* (1/171-185), *"Tafsir-ul-Baghawi"* (3/33), *"Fath-ul-Baari"* authored by Ibn Hajr (1/145,146), *"Zaad-ul-Museer"* authored by Ibn-ul-Jawzi' (4/359,360), and *"Tafsir-ul-Qaasimee"* (10/3727)

مَثَلُ الإيمانِ كَشَجَرَةٍ ، فَأَصْلُهَا الـشَّـهَادَةُ ، وَ سَاقُهَا وَ
وَرَقُهَا كَذَا ، وَ ثَمَرُهَا الْوَرعُ ، وَ لَا خَيْرَ فِي شَـجَرَةٍ لَا
ثَمَرَ لَهَا ، وَ لَا خَيْـرَ فِي إِنْـسَانٍ لَا وَرَعَ فِيهِ .

"The example of Eemaan is like a tree: its root is the shahada (testimony of faith); its trunk and leaves are so and so, and the fruit is al-wara' (piety, fearing Allâh). There is no goodness in a tree that bears no fruit, and there is no goodness in a person that does not possess al-wara'" 30

Al-Bagawi (may Allâh have mercy upon him) said:

وَ الْـحِكْمَةُ فِي تَمْثِيلِ الْإِيمَانِ بِالشَّجَرَةِ هِيَ أَنَّ
الـشَّجَرَةَ لَا تَكُونُ شَـجَرَةً إِلَّا بِثَلَاثَةِ أَشْيَاءَ ، عِرَقٌ
رَاسِخٌ ، وَ أَصْلٌ قَائِمٌ ، وَ فَرْعٌ عَالٍ ، وَ كَذَلِكَ الْإِيمَانُ لَا

SOME OF THE ASPECTS OF RESEMBLANCE BETWEEN THE DATE TREE AND THE BELIEVER

يَتِمُّ إِلَّا بِثَلَاثَةِ أَشْيَاءَ ، تَصْدِيقٌ بِالْقَلْبِ ، وَ قَوْلٌ بِاللَّسَانِ ، وَ عَمَلٌ بِالْأَبْدَانِ .

"The wisdom in comparing Eemaan with a tree is that a tree is not a tree without three things: strong roots, an upright trunk, and high branches and likewise Eemaan is not completed without three things: belief of the heart, speech of the tongue, and action of the limbs" [31]

Ibn Al-Qayyim said:

الْإِخْلَاصُ وَ التَّوْحِيدُ شَجَرَةٌ فِي الْقَلْبِ فُرُوعُهَا الْأَعْمَالُ ، وَ ثَمَرُهَا طِيبُ الْحَيَاةِ فِي الدُّنْيَا ، وَ النَّعِيمُ الْمُقِيمُ فِي الْآخِرَةِ ، وَ كَمَا أَنَّ ثِمَارَ الْجَنَّةِ لَا مَقْطُوعَةَ وَ لَا مَمْنُوعَةَ ، فَثَمَرَةُ التَّوْحِيدِ وَ الْإِخْلَاصِ فِي الدُّنْيَا كَذَلِكَ ، وَ الشِّرْكُ وَ الْكَذِبُ وَ الرِّيَاءُ شَجَرَةٌ

فِي الْقَلْبِ ثَمَرُهَا فِي الدُّنْيَا الْخَوْفُ وَ الْهَمُّ وَ الْغَمُّ

وَ ضِيقُ الصَّدَرِ وَ ظُلْمَةُ الْقَلْبِ، وَ ثَمَرُهَا فِي الْآخِرَةِ

الزَّقُومُ وَ الْعَذَابُ الْمُقِيمُ ، وَ قَدْ ذَكَرَ اللهُ هَاتَيْنِ

الشَّجَرَتَيْنِ فِي سُورَةِ إِبْرَاهِيمَ .

"Sincerity and Tawheed are a tree in the heart; its branches are righteous actions and its fruit are a good life in the Dunya and eternal bliss in the hereafter. Just as, the fruit of Jannah are uninterrupted by season and are limitless, then so too are the fruits of Tawheed and sincerity. Shirk, lying and Riya is a tree in the heart also, and the fruits in the Dunya are fear, sadness, tightening of the chest and darkening of the heart, and its fruit in the hereafter are the Zaqoom and never-ending punishment. Allah mentions both these trees in Soorah Ibrahim" [32]

The 2nd aspect:

---

[32] In the book *"Al-Fawaa'id"* (page 214-215)

45

SOME OF THE ASPECTS OF RESEMBLANCE BETWEEN THE DATE TREE AND THE BELIEVER

The date tree cannot live and will not grow without water. If it is left without water, then it will wither and if it is cut off entirely then it will die, so there is no life without water. The believer is also like this; he does not live a true life, and his life is not good unless his heart is watered with the revelation of the speech of Allâh and the speech of His messenger (may peace and blessings be upon him). This is the reason Allâh calls the revelation a Rûh (life, essence, etc.) In the verse:

﴿ وَكَذَٰلِكَ أَوْحَيْنَا إِلَيْكَ رُوحًا مِنْ أَمْرِنَا مَا كُنْتَ تَدْرِى مَا ٱلْكِتَبُ وَلَا ٱلْإِيمَٰنُ وَلَٰكِن جَعَلْنَٰهُ نُورًا نَهْدِى بِهِۦ مَن نَّشَآءُ مِنْ عِبَادِنَا ﴾

"And thus We have sent to you (O Muhammad may peace and blessings) Ruhan (an Inspiration, and a Mercy) of Our Command. You knew not what is the Book, nor what is Faith? But We have made it (this Qur'ân) a light wherewith We guide whosoever of Our slaves We will." [33]

---

[33] Ash-Shura [42:52]

And the verse:

$$﴿ يُنَزِّلُ ٱلْمَلَٰٓئِكَةَ بِٱلرُّوحِ مِنْ أَمْرِهِۦ عَلَىٰ مَن يَشَآءُ مِنْ عِبَادِهِۦٓ ﴾$$

**"He sends down the angels with the Rûh
(inspiration) of His Command to whom of His
slaves He pleases."'[34]**

The true life of the heart can only exist with it,
and without it a person would be dead, even if
he is one of the living, like Allâh says in His
verse:

$$﴿ أَوَمَن كَانَ مَيْتًا فَأَحْيَيْنَٰهُ وَجَعَلْنَا لَهُۥ نُورًا يَمْشِى بِهِۦ فِى ٱلنَّاسِ كَمَن$$
$$مَّثَلُهُۥ فِى ٱلظُّلُمَٰتِ لَيْسَ بِخَارِجٍ مِّنْهَا ﴾$$

**"Is he who was dead (without Faith by
ignorance and disbelief) and We gave him life
(by knowledge and Faith) and set for him a
light (of Belief) whereby he can walk amongst
men, like him who is in the darkness (of**

---

[34] An-Nahl [16:2]

**disbelief, polytheism and hypocrisy) from
which he can never come out?"**[35]

And His saying:

**"O you who believe! Answer Allâh (by obeying
Him) and (His) Messenger when he (may
peace and blessings be upon him) calls you to
that which will give you life"** [36]

There are many verses with this same meaning.

This is a clear resemblance between the believer
and the date tree. The date tree cannot live if it
is not given water and the heart of the believer
cannot live if it is not given revelation. If Allâh
sends down the rain upon the dead earth it is
affected, and every variety of splendor is brought
forth from it.

---

[35] Al-An'aam [6:122]
[36] Al-An'fal [8:24]

Similarly the dead heart when it hears the revelation and accepts it becomes rectified, proper, and much good grows inside it. Allâh in *Soorah Al-Hadid* warns from a lack of reverence for the mentioning of Allâh, like those who were given the book before and after a long time their hearts became hard. Allâh, the most glorified, says at the end of it:

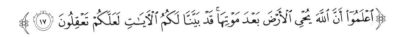

"Know that Allâh gives life to the earth after its death! Indeed We have made clear the Ayât (proofs, evidences, verses, lessons, signs, revelations, etc.) To you, if you but understand." [37]

This is an indication that the one that gives life to the earth also gives life to the hearts with revelation, but that is only for the one that understands Allâh's verses. This clarified as Ibn Al-Qayyim said, that:

---

[37] Al-Hadeed [57:17]

SOME OF THE ASPECTS OF RESEMBLANCE BETWEEN THE DATE TREE AND THE BELIEVER

"The tree of Islâm in the heart must be continually watered with beneficial knowledge, righteous actions, and by reflecting on past ideas to gain new benefits without which the tree would dry out and wither."

In the book *Musnad* by Imam Ahmad, from the hadith of Abu Hurayrah who said the Messenger of Allâh ﷺ (may peace and blessings be upon him) said:

$$ إِنَّ الْإِيمَانَ يُخْلَقُ فِي الْقَلْبِ كَمَا يُخْلَقُ الثَّوْبُ فَجَدِّدُوا إِيمَانَكُمْ $$

'Verily Eemaan is made in the heart just as a thowb is made so renew your Eemaan.' [38]

---

[38] Al-Hakim noted it (1/4) from the hadith of 'Abdillah Bin 'Umaru Bin Al-'Aas, may Allâh be pleased with them both, He said, "the messenger of Allâh (peace and blessing be upon him) said, **"Verily Eemaan is made in the heart of you all just like the thowb is made, So ask Allâh to renew your Eemaan."** And Al-Hakim said, "Its wording is from trustworthy men." And Adh-Dhahabi agrees. Also, At-Tabarani reported it in the book *"Al-*

In general the seedling is not diligently cared for;
then it is on the verge of perishing. From this,
you will understand the servants' extreme need
for whatever Allâh commanded from acts of
worship on a recurring basis, and it shows His
great mercy, complete blessings and beneficence
to His servants that He made the acts of worship
incumbent upon them, and He made them a
substance to water the seedling of Tawheed that
has been planted in their hearts. [39]

The 3rd aspect:

The date tree is extremely firm as Allâh said in
the previously mentioned verse:

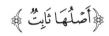

"Whose root is firmly fixed" [40]

Kabeer" just like the book *"Majma' Al-Zawa'id"* (1/52); and Al-
Haythamee said, "Its Isnaad is Hasan" and Al-Albaani
authenticated it. Look in the book *"Saheeh-ul-Jaamee"* (#159),
and in the book *"As-Silsila-tus-Saheehah"* (4/113)

[39] In the book *"I'laam Al-Muwaqi'een"* authored by Ibn Al-Qayyim
(1/174)

[40] Ibrahim [14:24]

SOME OF THE ASPECTS OF RESEMBLANCE BETWEEN THE DATE TREE AND THE BELIEVER

That is the case with *Eemaan* if it takes hold in the heart. It becomes so firm that nothing can shake it, like the firmly rooted mountains.

Al-Awza'i was asked whether *Eemaan* increases, he replied:

نَعَمْ حَتَّى يَكُونَ كَالْجِبَالِ ، قِيلَ : أَ يَنْقَصُ ؟ قَالَ :
نَعَمْ حَتَّى لَا يَبْقَى مِنْهُ شَيِئٌ .

"Yes, until it becomes like the mountains", then it was said: "Does it decrease?" He said: "Yes until nothing of it remains".[41]

Imam Ahmad was asked about the increase and decrease of *Eemaan;* he said:

يَزِيدُ حَتَّى يَبْلُغَ أَعْلَى السَّمَوَاتِ السَّبْعِ ، وَ يَنْقُصُ
حَتَّى يَصِيرَ إِلَى أَسْفَلَ السَّافِلِينَ السَّبْعِ .

---

[41] Al-Alkaa'I reported it in the book *"Sharh-ul-'Itiqaad"* (5/959)

"It increases until it reaches the highest of
the seven heavens and it decreases until it
reaches the lowest of the seven depths." [42]

The 4th aspect:
The date tree does not grow in every place.
Rather it only grows in specific areas with good
earth. So in some places it does not grow at all;
in some places it grows but does not bear any
fruit; in some places, it bears fruit, but of a bad
quality, so not, every place is suitable for the
date tree.

Abu Hatim As-Sijistani said:

قَالُواْ : وَ إِنَّمَا يَرْدِيهِ وَ يَسِيءُ نَبَتُهُ طَعَمَةَ الْأَرْضِ ،
فَيَجِيءُ ضَخْماً كَثِيرُ الْقِشْرِ ، سَرِيعُ الْيَبَسِ ثِنِتاً ،
أَيْ : عَفِناً ، جَخِراً نَخِراً ، وَ الْجَخِرُ : الضَّخْمُ الَّذِي
لَيْسَتْ لَهُ قَوَّةٌ وَ لَا تَعْجَبُهُ الْأَرْضُ فَيَمِيلُ وَ يَنْتَفِخُ وَ
تَخْوِي نَخْلَتُهُ وَ تَرْدُؤُ ، وَ إِذَا كَانَ فِي أَرْضٍ جَيِّدَةً

SOME OF THE ASPECTS OF RESEMBLANCE BETWEEN THE DATE TREE AND THE BELIEVER

السِّرِ جَاءَ أَبْيَضَ رَقِيقاً ، وَ تَرَاهُ كَأَنَّ طَرَفَهُ يَدْرِي لَا

يُعَوِّجُهُ شَيْءٌ حَتَّى يُدْرِكَ الْمَاءُ بَعُدَ أَوْ قَرُبَ ، وَ إِذَا

كَانَ الْعِرْقُ فِي أَرْضٍ طَيِّبَةِ الطِّينِ وَقَفَ سَاعَةً يَشْرَعُ

فِي الْمَاءِ ، لِأَنَّهُ يَرْجِعُ إِلَى طِينَةٍ طَيِّبَةٍ وَ طُعْمَةٍ

تَعْجَبُهُ ، وَ لَمْ يَنْحَدِرْ إِلَّا طَلَبَ الْمَاءَ ، فَلَمَّا شَامَ

الْمَاءَ وَقَفَ ، وَ إِذَا انْحَدَرَ مِنْ أَرْضٍ خَبِيثَةِ الطِّينِ

لَيْسَ لَهَا سِرٌّ انْخَرَطَ حَتَّى يَتَثَنَّى فِي الْمَاءِ عَفِناً ،

لِأَنَّهُ إِنَّمَا سَاقُهُ طَلَبُ الْمَاءِ ، فَلَمَّا وَجَدَ طُعْمَةَ

الْمَاءِ جَعَلَ انْخِرَاطاً فِيهِ مِنْ بُغْضِ مَا فَوْقَهُ .

"The taste of the earth i.e. The soil type that a tree is in being what makes a tree go bad i.e. rot, causing the tree to become thick, weak, smelly and finally dry out. The thickness in the tree when this happens is without strength and the tree loses its firm hold on the soil almost as if the earth has rejected it as it leans, becomes flaccid, falls and rots.

When the tree is in well tilled or loose earth with enough space for movement, its roots come out a tenuous white shooting out perpendicular to the tree, travelling in straight lines parallel to the earth until they sense water.

When the roots arrive at a well irrigated soil they then stay there with the water they have found. The reason for this is that the roots seek to return to a well-watered earth with a desired flavor and only move downwards in their search of water i.e. when the roots become submersed in water, they stop moving.

Then when the roots arrive at poorly irrigated soil without space for much movement they become thin and elongated to be able to penetrate the soil. This is because what drives the motion of the roots is their search for water. So when they find the taste of water beneath them better than the soil that they are in, they start to thin and elongate

**away from the poor soil, out of dislike for
that poor soil above them."** [43]

Therefore, not all soil is compatible with the date
tree.

This is the way of *Eemaan*; it does not become
firm in every heart. *Eemaan* only becomes firm
in the hearts of those that Allâh has written for
them guidance and has widened their chest for
Eemaan. The hearts are of different containers,
and in this regard Abu Musa Al-Ashari said that
messenger of Allâh ﷺ (may peace and
blessings be upon him) said:

مَثَلُ مَا بَعَثَنِي اللهُ بِهِ مِنَ الْهُدَى وَ الْعِلْمِ،، كَمَثَلِ

غَيْثٍ أَصَابَ الْأَرْضِ،، فَكَانَتْ مِنْهَا طَائِفَةٌ قَبِلَتِ

الْمَاءَ فَأَنْبَتَتِ الْكَلَأَ وَ الْعُشْبَ الْكَثِيرَ ، وَ كَانَتْ

مِنْهَا أَجَادِبَ قَدْ أَمْسَكَتِ الْمَاءَ فَنَفَعَ اللهُ بِهِ النَّاسَ

فَشَرِبُواْ مِنْهَا وَرَعُواْ وَ سَقُواْ ، وَ أَصَابَتْ طَائِفَةٌ أُخْرَى

---

[43] In the book *"Kitaab-un-Nakhl"* (page 66-67)

إِنَّمَا هِيَ قِيعَانٌ فَلَا تُمْسِكُ مَاءً وَ لَا تَنْبِتُ كَلَأً ،
كَذَلِكَ مَثَلِي وَ مَثَلُ مَنْ فَقَهَ فِي دِينِ اللهِ وَ نَفَعَهُ مَا
بَعَثَنِي اللهُ بِهِ فَعَلِمَ وَ عَلَّمَ ، وَ مَثَلُ مَنْ لَمْ يَرْفَعْ
بِذَلِكَ رَأْساً وَ لَمْ يَقْبَلْ هُدَى اللهِ الَّذِي أُرْسِلْتُ بِهِ .

"The example of that which Allâh sent me
with from guidance and knowledge is like
that of the heavy rains that pour down on the
earth. Some areas accept the rain and grow
pastures and vegetation. Some areas are
nonporous and hold the water, so Allâh
benefits the people with it, they drink from
it; they cultivate with it, and they irrigate
with it. Some areas are flat, so do not hold
the water and do not grow pastures. Similar
is my example, and the example of the one
that understands Allâh's religion and is
benefitted by that which I was sent with, so
he knows, and he teaches, and similar is the
example of the one who does not raise his
head or accept the guidance of Allâh that I
was sent with." [44]

---

[44] Saheeh-ul-Bukhari (1/45) and Saheeh Muslim (4/1787)

The 5ᵗʰ aspect:

The date tree can be surrounded by growth that harm the tree, hampers its growth, crowds it and takes from its irrigation. The date tree, therefore, requires a specific kind of routine maintenance by its owner to remove this harmful growth and vegetation. If he does this then his plant will reach its full growth, but if he is neglectful then the surrounding growth could overcome his plant and weaken the roots.

This is also the case with the believer; there is no doubt that he is accompanied in this life by things that can weaken his *Eemaan* and his certainty, and crowd the roots of *Eemaan* that are in the heart. The believer, therefore, must always strive to take account of himself and to work hard to remove every source of evil on the heart and to distance himself from everything that has a bad influence on the state of *Eemaan* like the whispers of the *Shaytan,* or the soul that is built upon bad, or the *Dunya* with its trials and temptations, etc. Allâh says:

﴿ وَٱلَّذِينَ جَٰهَدُواْ فِينَا لَنَهْدِيَنَّهُمْ سُبُلَنَا ۚ وَإِنَّ ٱللَّهَ لَمَعَ ٱلْمُحْسِنِينَ ٦٩ ﴾

"As for those who strive hard in Us (Our Cause), We will surely guide them to Our Paths (i.e. Allâh's Religion - Islâmic Monotheism). And verily, Allâh is with the Muhsinun (good doers)". [45]

The 6th aspect:

The date tree, as Allâh informs us:

﴿ تُؤْتِىٓ أُكُلَهَا كُلَّ حِينٍ ﴾

"Giving its fruit at all times..." [46]

Its food is its fruit, and it produces its fruit all the time, be it night or day, summer or winter, either it produces a *tamr* (dried date), or *busr* (unripe dates), or *rutb* (fresh date). Likewise, the actions of the believer are risen up at the

---

[45] Al-Ankabut [29:69]

[46] Ibrahim [14:25]

beginning and end of the night. Rabi' bin Anas
said in explanation of:

"...At all times..."

Meaning: *every morning and night, because the
fruit of the date tree is eaten night and day,
summer and winter, whether it be tamr, rutb, or
busr. Likewise, the actions of the believers rise up
at the beginning and end of every night."* [47]

Ad-Dhahak said:

$$ ﴿ تُؤْتِى أُكُلَهَا كُلَّ حِينٍ ﴾ $$

"Giving its fruit at all times..."

"It brings out its fruit all the time, and this is
like the believer: he performs righteous actions
all the time, every hour of the day and night,

---

[47] Al-Baghawi mentioned it in his Tafsir (3/33)

winter and summer, in the obedience of Allâh."
48

Ibn Jarir narrated a number of sayings of the
Salaf in regards to the meaning of Allâh's saying:
"...At all times..." Then he said:

*"The foremost of the sayings in my opinion is the
one who said: The meaning of "time" in this place
is the morning and evening and every hour
because Allâh mentions the produce of this tree
that comes all the time as a parable for the
actions of the believer and there is no doubt that
righteous speech and actions are sent up to Allâh
every day, not every year or every six months or
bimonthly. Therefore, if this is correct then there
is no doubt that the thing being compared cannot
contradict the thing that it is being compared to in
its meaning. So of, it is like that then the accuracy
of what I have said should be clear. If someone
was to say: 'What kind of date tree produces fruit
all the time, summer and winter?', then it is said
to them that, in the winter, the flowers are from
its fruit and in the summer you have the dates,
the unripe dates, the fresh dates, and the dried*

---

48 Ibn Jarir reported it in his Tafsir (8/208)

dates, and all of that is from the fruit of the date tree." [49]

It is reported from Qatada he said:

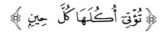

"Giving its fruit at all times..."

Meaning: its fruit is eaten in the winter and summer.

The 7th aspect:

The date tree has blessings in every part of it. There is no part of it that cannot be benefitted from. This is also the way of the believer as is narrated in *Saheeh Al-Bukhari* in one of the variations of the hadith of Ibn Umarb; that preceded, from the narration of Al-A'mash upon the authority of Mujahid, upon the authority of Ibn Umar, that the Prophet ﷺ (may peace and blessings be upon him) said:

---

[49] In the book Tafsir At-Tabari (8/210)

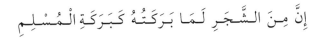

"Verily there is a tree that has been blessed like the blessing of the Muslim..."

Ibn Hajar said about this hadith:

"The blessing of the date tree is found in every part of it and is continuous throughout its different states so from whenever it produces fruit till when they dry, they can be eaten in different ways. The rest of the tree can also be used: including the date stones for feeding livestock, the fibers for making rope, and many other well-known uses. Likewise, the blessing of the Muslim encompasses every situation, and his benefit to himself and to others continues even after his death.""[50]

The 8ᵗʰ aspect:

The date tree, as the Prophet ﷺ (may peace and blessings be upon him) described it,

---

[50] In the book authored by Ibn Hajr *"Fath-ul-Baari"* (1/145-146)

"doesn't lose its leaves", and the resemblance between the believer and the date tree in this respect is made apparent by the saying of Al-Harith bin Abi Usamah in the hadith of a different wording on the authority of Ibn Umar:

كُنَّا عِنْدَ رَسُولِ الله – صَلَّى اللهُ عَلَيْهِ وَ سَلَّمَ – ذَاتَ يَوْمٍ

فَقَالَ : إِنَّ مَثَلَ الْمُؤْمِنِ كَمَثَلِ شَجَرَةٍ لَا تَسْقُطُ لَهَا

أَنْمِلَةٌ ، أَ تَدْرُونَ مَا هِيَ ؟ قَالُوا : لَا . قَالَ : هِيَ

النَّخْلَةُ ، لَا تَسْقُطُ لَهَا أَنْمِلَةٌ ، وَ لَا تَسْقُطُ لِمُؤْمِنٍ

دَعْوَةٌ .

"We were with the Messenger of Allâh (may peace and blessings of Allâh be upon him) one day and he said: 'Verily the example of the believer is like that of a tree that does not lose its leaves, do you know what it is?', we said: no, so he said: 'It is the date tree: it does not lose its leaves and likewise the believer's dua (supplication) is never lost.'" 51

---

51 In the book authored by Ibn Hajr *"Fath-ul-Baari"* (1 / 145)

Al-Qurtubi made clear the importance of this addition and its great benefit when he said in his *Tafsir*:

"Al-Harith bin Usama's addition was equal to a journey to the Prophet ﷺ (may peace and blessings be upon him), he said: 'It is the date tree: its leaves do not fall and likewise the believer's dua is never lost.', So he clarifies the meaning of the hadith and the resemblance between them." [52]

Dua is what we have been ordered with, and its acceptance has been guaranteed, just as Allâh, the most high says:

$$﴿ وَقَالَ رَبُّكُمُ ٱدْعُونِيٓ أَسْتَجِبْ لَكُمْ ﴾$$

"And your Lord said: "Invoke Me, [i.e. Believe in My Oneness (Islâmic Monotheism)] (and ask Me for anything) I will respond to your (invocation)."[53]

---

[52] In the book *"Al-Jaami Li Ah-kaam-ul-Quran"* (9/236)
[53] Ghaafir [40:60]

SOME OF THE ASPECTS OF RESEMBLANCE
BETWEEN THE DATE TREE AND THE
BELIEVER

Although the *dua* is only a cause and requisite for acceptance if the conditions are complete and the obstacles are removed, the acceptance of the dua could be different due to the absence of some of the conditions or the presence of some of the obstacles and its etiquettes. The greatest of the etiquettes of *dua* is the presence of the heart, hope of acceptance, and determination upon the affair.

Ibn Al-Qayyim mentioned in regards to the meaning of the hadith another viewpoint, and that is:

"The continuation of its covering and its beauty that never changes summer or winter is like the believer who is never without the covering of Taqwâ (righteousness) and its beauty until Allâh calls him back." [54]

The 9ᵗʰ aspect:

---

[54] In the book *"Miftaah Daar-us-Saa'da"* (1/116)

The date tree was described in the verse as
"goodly", and this encompasses more than just
the good look or shape, the good smell, fruit, and
benefit. The most honorable characteristic of the
believer is his goodness in all his affairs and
every situation; in that which is apparent and
that which is hidden, in secret and in public.
Because of this when the believers enter heaven,
and they are met by its keepers they say to
them:

﴾ سَلَٰمٌ عَلَيۡكُمۡ طِبۡتُمۡ فَٱدۡخُلُوهَا خَٰلِدِينَ ۝ ﴿

**"Salâmun 'Alaikum (peace be upon you)! You
were good, so enter here to abide therein."** [55]

And Allâh, the Most High says:

﴾ ٱلَّذِينَ تَتَوَفَّىٰهُمُ ٱلۡمَلَٰٓئِكَةُ طَيِّبِينَ يَقُولُونَ سَلَٰمٌ عَلَيۡكُمُ ٱدۡخُلُوا ٱلۡجَنَّةَ بِمَا
كُنتُمۡ تَعۡمَلُونَ ۝ ﴿

---

[55] Az-Zumar [39:73]

SOME OF THE ASPECTS OF RESEMBLANCE BETWEEN THE DATE TREE AND THE BELIEVER

"Those whose lives the angels take while they are in a pious state (i.e. Pure from all evil, and worshipping none but Allâh Alone) saying (to them): Salâmun 'Alaikum (peace be on you) enter you Paradise, because of (the good) which you used to do (in the world)." [56]

And He, the most high says,

﴿ إِنَّ ٱللَّهَ يُدْخِلُ ٱلَّذِينَ ءَامَنُوا۟ وَعَمِلُوا۟ ٱلصَّٰلِحَٰتِ جَنَّٰتٍ تَجْرِى مِن تَحْتِهَا ٱلْأَنْهَٰرُ يُحَلَّوْنَ فِيهَا مِنْ أَسَاوِرَ مِن ذَهَبٍ وَلُؤْلُؤًا۟ وَلِبَاسُهُمْ فِيهَا حَرِيرٌ ۝ وَهُدُوٓا۟ إِلَى ٱلطَّيِّبِ مِنَ ٱلْقَوْلِ وَهُدُوٓا۟ إِلَىٰ صِرَٰطِ ٱلْحَمِيدِ ۝ ﴾

"Truly, Allâh will admit those who believe (in the Oneness of Allâh Islâmic Monotheism) and do righteous good deeds, to Gardens underneath, which rivers flow (in Paradise), wherein they will be adorned with bracelets of gold and pearls and their garments therein will be of silk; And they are guided (in this

---

[56] An-Nahl [16:32]

world) unto goodly speech (i.e. Lâ ilâha ill-
Allâh, Alhamdu lillâh, recitation of the
Qur'ân, etc.), And they are guided to the Path
of Him (i.e. Allâh's Religion of Islâmic
Monotheism), Who is Worthy of all praises. [57]

Goodness is the most dignified of their
characteristics, most beautiful of their
descriptions, and the best of their adornments
for every situation, every statement, every
action, every movement, every stillness, and
every one of their affairs.

The 10th aspect:

The date tree is described, in the hadith of Ibn
Umar that proceeded, with that: "whatever you
take from it will benefit you", and Ibn Al-Qayyim
said:

**"The entire date tree is beneficial; nothing
falls from it without a benefit. Its fruit is
beneficial; its trunk has a number of benefits,
that are well known for buildings, roofing,
etc.; Its leaves can be used to cover a roof in**

---

[57] Al-Hajj [22:23-24]

place of reeds and to cover openings and holes; its wicker is used for baskets, pouches, types of containers, mats, etc.; And its bark and its fronds have uses that are known to the people"[58]

This is also the way of the believer with his brothers, companions, and fellow travelers; they do not see anything but honorable characteristics, supreme manners, excellent dealings, advice and good deeds for his companions. They do not experience any harm from him; rather they do not experience anything but benefit, like a good speech, or sermon, beautiful characteristics, aid and help, and so forth. Therefore, he is like the date tree: whatever you take from him is beneficial to you.

The 11ᵗʰ aspect:

There is a lot of difference between the date trees, difference in the look, the type, and the fruit. The date trees are not all on the same level

---

[58] In the book *"Miftaah Daar-us-Sa'adah"* authored by Ibn Al-Qayyim (1/120)

of beauty and quality, rather there is a big disproportion and differentiation between them, as Allâh, the most High, says:

وَفِي ٱلْأَرْضِ قِطَعٌ مُّتَجَٰوِرَٰتٌ وَجَنَّٰتٌ مِّنْ أَعْنَٰبٍ وَزَرْعٌ وَنَخِيلٌ صِنْوَانٌ وَغَيْرُ صِنْوَانٍ يُسْقَىٰ بِمَآءٍ وَٰحِدٍ وَنُفَضِّلُ بَعْضَهَا عَلَىٰ بَعْضٍ فِي ٱلْأُكُلِ إِنَّ فِي ذَٰلِكَ لَءَايَٰتٍ لِّقَوْمٍ يَعْقِلُونَ ٤

"And in the earth are neighboring tracts, and gardens of vines, and green crops (fields etc.), And date-palms, growing out two or three from a single stem root, or otherwise (one stem root for every palm), watered with the same water, yet some of them We make more excellent than others to eat. Verily, in these things, there are Ayât (proofs, evidences, lessons, signs) for the people who understand." [59]

So it differs in its taste, look, and type; and some are better than others.

---

[59] Ar-Ra'd [13:4]

SOME OF THE ASPECTS OF RESEMBLANCE BETWEEN THE DATE TREE AND THE BELIEVER

This is also the case between the believers, so the believers differ in *Eemaan* and are not all on one level, rather there is a large disproportion between them and some are better than others. Allâh, the Most High, says:

$$﴿ ثُمَّ أَوْرَثْنَا الْكِتَابَ الَّذِينَ اصْطَفَيْنَا مِنْ عِبَادِنَا فَمِنْهُمْ ظَالِمٌ لِنَفْسِهِ وَمِنْهُم مُّقْتَصِدٌ وَمِنْهُمْ سَابِقٌ بِالْخَيْرَاتِ بِإِذْنِ اللَّهِ ذَلِكَ هُوَ الْفَضْلُ الْكَبِيرُ ﴿٣٢﴾ ﴾$$

"Then We gave the Book the Qur'ân) for inheritance to such of Our slaves whom We chose (the followers of Muhammad, may peace, and blessings be upon him). Then of them are some who wrong their own selves, and of them are some who follow a middle course, and of them are some who are, by Allâh's Leave, foremost in good deeds. That (inheritance of the Qur'ân) that is indeed a great grace." [60]

---

[60] Fatir [35:32]

The 12th aspect:

The date tree is one of the most resilient trees against the wind and strain. The other large trees are sometimes bent by the wind, sometimes they are uprooted, and their branches are broken. Most of them have no resilience for a lack of water like that of the date tree.

The believer is also most patient in the face of hardship and is not shaken by the wind. The three types of patience are combined in the believer: patience upon obedience to Allâh; patience upon ones sins; and patience upon the difficulties that have been pre-decreed. Allâh the most high says:

﴿ وَبَشِّرِ ٱلصَّٰبِرِينَ ۝ ٱلَّذِينَ إِذَآ أَصَٰبَتْهُم مُّصِيبَةٌ قَالُوٓاْ إِنَّا لِلَّهِ وَإِنَّآ إِلَيْهِ رَٰجِعُونَ ۝ أُوْلَٰٓئِكَ عَلَيْهِمْ صَلَوَٰتٌ مِّن رَّبِّهِمْ وَرَحْمَةٌ وَأُوْلَٰٓئِكَ هُمُ ٱلْمُهْتَدُونَ ۝ ﴾

"...And give glad tidings to As-Sâbirin (the patient ones, etc.). Who, when afflicted with

73

calamity, say: "Truly! To Allâh we belong and
truly, to Him we shall return." They are those
on whom are the Salawât (i.e. Blessings, etc.)
(i.e. Who are blessed and will be forgiven)
from their Lord, and (they are those who)
receive His Mercy, and it is they who are the
guided-ones." [61]

And He, the Most High says:

﴿ قُلْ يَٰعِبَادِ ٱلَّذِينَ ءَامَنُوا۟ ٱتَّقُوا۟ رَبَّكُمْ لِلَّذِينَ أَحْسَنُوا۟ فِى هَٰذِهِ ٱلدُّنْيَا حَسَنَةٌ
وَأَرْضُ ٱللَّهِ وَٰسِعَةٌ إِنَّمَا يُوَفَّى ٱلصَّٰبِرُونَ أَجْرَهُم بِغَيْرِ حِسَابٍ ۝ ﴾

"Say (O Muhammad, may peace and blessings
be upon him): "O My slaves who believe (in
the Oneness of Allâh Islâmic Monotheism), be
afraid of your Lord (Allâh) and keep your duty
to Him. Good is (the reward) for those who do
good in this world, and Allâh's earth is
spacious (so if you cannot worship Allâh at a
place, then go to another)! Only those who

---

[61] Al-Baqarah [2:155-157]

are patient shall receive their rewards in full,
without reckoning." [62]

The 13th aspect:

As the date tree ages, it increases in goodness
and its fruit improves in quality and likewise the
believer if his life is long he increases in
goodness and his deeds improve.

At-Tirmidhi reports on the authority of Abdullah
bin Busr that a Bedouin man said:

يَا رَسُولَ اللهِ مَنْ خَيْرُ النَّاسِ؟ قَالَ : ((مَنْ طَالَ عُمْرُهُ وَ
حَسُنَ عَمَلُهُ)).

**"O Messenger of Allâh who is the best of the
people?" He said: "Whoever's life is long and
his deeds are good."** [63]

He also reported on the authority of Abu Bakra
that a man said:

---

62 Az-Zumar [39:10]

63 Sunan At-Tirmidhi (4/565) and Al-Albani authenticated it in
his book *"Saheeh Sunan At-Tirmidhi"* (2/271)

SOME OF THE ASPECTS OF RESEMBLANCE
BETWEEN THE DATE TREE AND THE
BELIEVER

يَا رَسُولَ الله أَيُّ النَّاسِ خَيْرٌ ؟ قَالَ : ((مَنْ طَالَ عُمْرُهُ وَ

حَسُنَ عَمَلُهُ)) . قَالَ : فَأَيُّ النَّاسِ شَرٌّ ؟ قَالَ : ((مَنْ

طَالَ عُمْرُهُ وَ سَاءَ عَمَلُهُ)) .

**"O Messenger of Allâh which of the people are
the best?" He said: "Whoever's life is long and
his deeds are good." The man then said:
"Which of the people are the worst?" He said:
"Whoever's life is long and his deeds are
wicked." [64]**

Imam Ahmad and An-Nisa'i reported on the
subject of *"actions of the day and night"*, with a
"good" chain of narration, on the authority of
Abdullah bin Shaddad

أَنَّ نَفَراً مِنْ بَنِي عُذْرَةَ ثَلاثَةً أَتَوْا النَّبِيَّ - صَلَّى اللهُ

عَلَيْهِ وَ سَلَّمَ - فَأَسْلَمُوا قَالَ : فَقَالَ النَّبِيُّ - صَلَّى

---

[64] Sunan At-Tirmidhi (4/566) and Al-Albaani authenticated it
in his book *"Saheeh Sunan At-Tirmidhi"* (2/271)

اللهُ عَلَيْهِ وَ سَلَّمَ : ((مَنْ يَكْفِينِيهُمْ)) قَالَ طَلْحَةُ :
أَنَا ، قَالَ : فَكَانُوا عِنْدَ طَلْحَةَ فَبَعَثَ النَّبِيُّ - صَلَّى
اللهُ عَلَيْهِ بَعْثاً فَخَرَجَ فِيهِ أَحَدُهُمْ فَاسْتُشْهِدَ ، قَالَ :
ثُمَّ بَعَثَ بَعْثاً آخَرَ، فَخَرَجَ فِيهِمْ آخَرُ فَاسْتُشْهِدَ ،
قَالَ : ثُمَّ مَاتَ الثَّالِثُ عَلَى فَرَاشِهِ ، قَالَ طَلْحَةُ :
فَرَأَيْتُ الْمَيِّتَ عَلَى فَرَاشِهِ أَمَامَهُمْ ، وَ رَأَيْتُ الَّذِي
اسْتُشْهِدَ أَخِيراً يَلِيهِ ، وَ رَأَيْتُ الَّذِي اسْتُشْهِدَ أَوَّلَهُمْ
آخَرَهُمْ ، قَالَ : فَدَخَلَنِي مِنْ ذَلِكَ ، قَالَ : فَأَتَيْتُ
النَّبِيَّ - صَلَّى اللهُ عَلَيْهِ وَ سَلَّمَ - فَذَكَرْتُ ذَلِكَ لَهُ ،
قَالَ : فَقَالَ رَسُولُ الله - صَلَّى اللهُ عَلَيْهِ وَ سَلَّمَ - : ((مَا
أَنْكَرْتَ مِنْ ذَلِكَ ، لَيْسَ أَحَدٌ أَفْضَلَ عِنْدَ الله مِنْ
مُؤْمِنٍ يُعَمَّرُ فِي الْإِسْلَامِ يَكْثُرُ تَكْبِيرُهُ وَ تَسْبِيحُهُ وَ
تَهْلِيلُهُ وَ تَحْمِيدُهُ.

"That a group of three people from the Udhra tribe came to the Prophet ﷺ **(may peace and blessings be upon him) and became**

77

SOME OF THE ASPECTS OF RESEMBLANCE
BETWEEN THE DATE TREE AND THE
BELIEVER

Muslim, then the Prophet ﷺ (may peace
and blessings be upon him) said: "Who will be
their host?" So Talhah said: "I will.". So they
were with Talhah when the Prophet ﷺ
(may peace and blessings be upon him) sent
out an army and one of the three went with
them and was martyred. Then he sent out
another army and another of the group went
with them and was also martyred. The third
remaining member of the group then died in
his bed. Talhah said: "I saw those three that
stayed with me, in Jannah, so I saw the one
who died on his bed in front of them and the
one who was martyred last behind him and
the one that was martyred first was the last
of them. This bothered me, so I went to the
Prophet (may peace and blessings be upon
him), and I mentioned that to him, so he
said: "What do you not believe from that?
There is no one better with Allâh than a
believer that lives long in Islam and says the
Takbeer (Allâh Akbar), the Tasbeeh
(subhanallah), tahleel (to say la ilaha illallah),
and the Tamheed (alhamdulillah) a lot." 65

---

65 In the book *"Al-Musnad"* (1/163) and the book *"As-Sunan Al-*

78

The 14th aspect:

The heart of the date tree, known as the *jummar* is one of the best and sweetest of the different types of hearts, and as we have already mentioned in some of the narrations of the hadith of Ibn Umar that proceeded

أَنَّ النَّبِيَّ - صَلَّى اللهُ عَلَيْهِ وَ سَلَّمَ - أُتِيَ بِجُمَّارٍ وَ : شَرَعَ فِي أَكْلِهِ ثُمَّ قَالَ : إِنَّ مِنَ الشَّجَرِ شَجَرَةٌ مَثَلُهَا كَمَثَلِ الْمُسْلِمِ

"That the Prophet ﷺ (may peace and blessings be upon him) was brought a jummar (date tree heart), and he quickly ate it, then he said: 'There is from the types of trees a tree; its example is like that of the Muslim"

The *jummar* of the date tree has a sweet flavor and a beautiful taste, and it is one of the best and nicest of hearts. Likewise, the heart of the

Kubra'" by An-Nisaaee' in the book of **"deeds done in the day and evening"** (#10674) and Al-Albaani graded it to be Hasan in his book *"As-Saheehah"* (#654)

believer is the best and nicest of hearts. It only carries goodness, and it does not hide anything but uprightness (*Istiqaamah*) and rectification.

The 15th aspect:

The benefit of the date tree is never entirely impaired; rather if a particular benefit is impaired then there are other benefits. So, even if it did not bear fruit one year then there would still be in it benefit and purpose for the people in its palm leaves, its fibers, and its fronds. This is how the believer is: he is never devoid of good character, rather if he is deficient in one respect then he makes up for it in another, so his goodness is always expected and the people are always safe from his evil. At-Tirmidhi narrated on the authority of the Prophet ﷺ (may peace and blessings be upon him) that he said:

خَيْرُكُمْ مَنْ يُرْجَى خَيْرُهُ وَ يُؤْمَنُ شَرُّهُ ، وَ شَرُّكُمْ مَنْ
لَا يُرْجَى خَيْرُهُ وَ لَا يُؤْمَنُ شَرُّهُ.

"The best of you is the one whose goodness is expected and everyone is safe from his evil and the worst of you is the one whom you do not expect good from and you are not safe from his evil." [66]

Due to that it is narrated on the authority of Ikramah in regards to the saying of Allâh, The Most High: *"...Like a goodly tree..."* He said:

$$ هِيَ النَّخْلَةُ لَا تَزَالُ فِيهَا مَنْفَعَةٌ $$

"It is the date tree which never ceases to have a benefit."" [67]

This is the way of the believer, like the date tree, he never ceases to have benefit, or rather benefits, and that is determined by his portion of *Eemaan.*

The 16ᵗʰ aspect:

---

[66] Sunan At-Tirmidhi (#2263) and Shaykh Al-Albaani authenticated it in his book *"Saheeh-ul-Jaami'"* (#332)
[67] Ibn Jarir reported it in his Tafsir (8/205)

It is easy to attain the fruit of the date tree as it is either short so, therefore, does not require the person to climb it, or it has outstretched branches making it easy to climb in comparison to other tall trees. So you will find it as if it is a staircase or a ladder leading to the top of it. The believer is also like this: his good is easy and close for whoever wishes to experience it without naivety or depravity.

The 17th aspect:

Its fruits are amongst the most beneficial of the fruits worldwide as its fresh fruits are eaten as a fruit and as a dessert. Its dried fruit is eaten as a daily staple, a soup, and also as a fruit. It is used to produce vinegar and sugar and is used in medicines and drinks. Its general usefulness is apparent, and this is the way of the believer in regard to his general benefits, various righteous acts and goodness.

Just as, the fruit of the date tree has a sweet taste, then likewise *Eemaan* has a sweetness also that cannot be tasted except with the

correct *Eemaan*. This is why he (may peace and
blessings be upon him) said:

ثَلَاثٌ مَنْ كُنَّ فِيهِ وَجَدَ بِهِنَّ حَلَاوَةَ الْإِيـمَانِ : أَنْ يَكُونَ
اللهُ وَ رَسُولُـهُ أَحَبَّ إِلَيْهِ مِمَّا سِوَاهُمَا ، وَ أَنْ يَـحِبَّ
الْـمَرْءُ لَا يَـحِبُّ إِلَّا لله ، وَ أَنْ يَكْرَهَ أَنْ يَـعُودَ فِي الْكُفْـرِ
كَـمَا يَكْرَهُ أَنْ يُـقْذَفَ فِي الـنَّارِ

**"There are three things if present in a person
then he will find the sweetness of Eemaan:
that Allâh and His messenger are more
beloved to him than anything else; that he
loves a person, and he only loves him for the
sake of Allâh; and that he hates to return to
disbelief just as he would hate to be thrown
into the fire."** [68]

Abu Muhammad bin Abi Jumrah said:

إِنَّمَا عَبَّرَ بِالْحَلَاوَةِ لِأَنَّ اللهَ شَبَّهَ الْإِيمَانَ بِالشَّجَرَةِ فِي قَوْلِهِ تَعَالَى : ﴿مَثَلًا كَلِمَةً طَيِّبَةً كَشَجَرَةٍ طَيِّبَةٍ﴾ فَالْكَلِمَةُ هِيَ كَلِمَةُ الْإِخْلَاصِ ، وَ الشَّجَرَةُ أَصْلُ الْإِيمَانِ ، وَ أَغْصَانُهَا اتِّبَاعُ الْأَمْرِ وَ اجْتِنَابُ النَّهِي ، وَ وَرَقُهَا مَا يَهْتِمُّ بِهِ الْمُؤْمِنُ مِنَ الْخَيْرِ ، وَ ثَمَرُهَا الطَّاعَاتُ ، وَ حَلَاوَةُ الثَّمَرِ جَنِي الثَّمَرَةِ ، وَ غَايَةُ كِمَالِهِ تَنَاهِي نَضْجُ الثَّمَرَةِ وَ بِهِ تَظْهَرُ حَلَاوَتُهَا .

"Verily he only used the word 'sweetness' because Allâh likened Eemaan to a tree in His, the Most High's saying: "...A parable - A goodly word as a goodly tree...", So the word is the word of Ikhlaas (sincerity); the tree is the foundation of Eemaan; its branches are following orders and distancing oneself from that which is forbidden; its leaves are that which the believer gave importance to in regards to good deeds; its fruit are the acts of obedience; the sweetness of the fruit is the reaping of fruits, and completeness of

Eemaan achieves the utmost ripeness of the fruit which brings out the sweetness." [69]

The 18th aspect:

The most exquisite thing that was mentioned around the juxtaposition of the characteristics of the different parts of the date tree and the characteristics of the believer is that which Ibn Al-Qayyim mentioned when he said:

"And some of the people matched these benefits with the characteristics of the Muslim, so they made for every benefit of the date tree a characteristic of the Muslim to match it. So when they come to the thorns of the date tree they make it, with its counterpart from the Muslim, the characteristic of severity upon the enemies of Allâh and the people of wickedness, so they are severe and harsh with them like the thorns and with the believers and the pious they are like the ripe dates in sweetness and softness: "...Severe against disbelievers, and merciful among themselves..." [70]

---

[69] In the book *"Fath-ul-Baari"* by Ibn Hajr (1/60)

[70] In the book *"Miftaah Daar-us-Sa'aadah"* (1/120-121)

ASPECTS OF THE TREE OF EEMAAN

These are some of the points of resemblance between the believer and the date tree. Some of the commentators mentioned other points of resemblance, but they are weak and in some cases baseless. Al-Hafidh Ibn Hajar mentions this in summary in his book "*Fath-ul-Bari*", he said:

"As for those who claim that the point of resemblance between the Muslim and the date tree is that if its head is cut off then it will die; or that it will not bear fruit unless it is pollinated; or that it will die if drowned in water; or that its pollen has the scent like that of human semen; or that it couples; or that it drinks from its top. All of these points are weak because these are all characteristics that are shared by human beings and are not specific to the Muslim. Weaker than that is the opinion of those who claim the date tree was created from the leftover clay of Adam as the hadith in that regard is not strong, and Allâh knows best." [71]

---

[71] In the book *"Fath-ul-Baari"* (1 / 147)

With that, which has proceeded, it is known that *Eemaan* is a blessed tree of immense benefit, abundant usefulness, and many fruits. It has a specific place that it grows in; it has a specific drink, and it has a trunk, branches and fruit.

As for its place then it is in the heart of the Muslim. Its seeds, trunk, limbs, and branches are placed in the heart.

As for its drink then it is the clear revelation: the book of Allâh and the *Sunnah* of the Messenger. The tree is watered by it, and without it the tree has no life and cannot grow.

As for its trunk: then it is the six foundations of *Eemaan*, the highest of which is the belief in Allâh, the Most High, so it is the foundation of the foundations of this blessed tree.

As for its branches: then it is the righteous actions, the various acts of obedience, and the numerous acts of *qurba* (an act that draws a person closer to Allâh) that the believer performs.

As for the fruit: then it is every bit of good and happiness that the believer attains in this life and the hereafter, so it is a fruit from the fruit of *Eemaan* and a result from its results.

The eminent scholar Abdurahman As-Sa'di wrote a nice treatise on this topic called *"The Explanation and Clarification of the Tree of Eemaan"*. In it, he brings the most important information of this blessed tree of *Eemaan*. He started his treatise, may Allâh have mercy upon him, with an explanation of *Eemaan* and a clarification of its definition. Secondly, he continued by mentioning its foundation, its assets, and from that which it derives. Thirdly, he mentioned its benefits and fruit. He continues on in that way, may Allâh have mercy upon him, from the previous noble verse that contains the comparison of the statement of *Eemaan* in the heart of the believer, which is the best of statements, with the date tree, which is the best of trees. Then he says:

"This tree varies greatly in the hearts of the believers depending on the level that it possesses of the characteristics that Allâh

describes it with. **Therefore, it is upon the
successful servant to rush to know about it,
and its characteristics, its reasons, its
foundations, and its branches and he must
strive to apply it theoretically and
practically, for verily his portion of goodness,
success, and instant and delayed happiness
are dependent on his portion of this tree."** [72]

The best explanation for the foundation and the
branches of this tree is the well-known hadith of
the branches of *Eemaan* that was reported by
Bukhari, Muslim and others from the hadith of
Abu Hurayrah, that the Prophet ﷺ (may
peace and blessings be upon him) said:

الْإِيمَانُ بِضْعٌ وَ سَبْعُونَ شُعْبَةً ، أَعْلَاهَا قَوْلُ لَا إِلَهَ إِلَّا

اللهُ ، وَ أَدْنَاهَا إِمَاطَةُ الْأَذَى عَنِ الطَّرِيقِ ، وَ الْحَيَاءُ

شُعْبَةٌ مِنْ شُعَبِ الْإِيمَانِ .

---

[72] In the book *"The Explanation and Clarification of the Tree of
Eemaan"* authored by Ibn Sa'dee (page 6-7)

"Eemaan is seventy odd branches, the highest of which is the statement: 'There is none worthy of worship except Allâh, and the lowest of which is to remove a hardship from the pathway, and shyness is one of the branches of Eemaan."

This hadith contains the best explanation of this blessed tree: its foundation, and its branches whether it is performed by the heart, the tongue or the limbs. This is the reason the imam Ibn Mundah, may Allâh have mercy upon him, said in his book "*Al-Eemaan*" after he related the previously mentioned hadith of Ibn Umar that contains the resemblance between the believer and the date tree:

"...Then the Prophet ﷺ (may peace and blessings be upon him) explained Eemaan with his Sunnah. When he understood Allâh's parable he then informed us that Eemaan has branches, the highest of which is the saying: 'There's none worthy of worship except Allâh, so he made the foundation of Eemaan

acceptance with the heart and tongue and made its branches the actions." [73]

A number of commentators of this hadith strove to count these branches and tried to limit them. They wrote on the subject many books, short and long, and they followed various methodologies. The best of which was that of Ibn Hiban (may Allâh have mercy upon him) he used a methodology that was unique and rare and required a lot of time and hard work. He said in the description of his methodology:

"I studied the meaning of the narration for a long time as our doctrine is that the Prophet ﷺ (may peace and blessings be upon him) never spoke without benefit, and there is nothing from his Sunnah that we do not understand what he meant. I began to count the acts of obedience from Eemaan, and I found that they were a lot more than the number, so I returned to the Sunnah and I counted the acts that the Messenger counted as from I and I found that the amount was less than the seventy odd, so I returned to

---

73 In the book *"Al-Eemaan"* (2/350)

that which covers that from the speech of our Lord and I recited it verse for verse with contemplation, and I counted all that Allâh, the Most Venerable, the Most High counted as from Eemaan, and I found that it was less than the seventy odd, so I added what was in The Book to the Sunnah, and I removed the repetitions, and I found that everything that Allâh, the Most Venerable, the Most High, counted as from Eemaan in His book and every act of obedience that the Messenger of Allâh, may peace and blessings be upon him, made from Eemaan in his sunnah was seventy nine branches with no addition or subtraction in any way. I therefore, knew that what was meant by the Prophet, may peace and blessings be upon him, in the narration was that Eemaan is seventy odd branches in The Book and the Sunnah. I discussed this completely with mention of its branches in the book 'The Description of Eemaan and its Branches', I hope it may be indispensable for the one who contemplates it, and so there is no need to repeat it in this book." [74]

---

[74] In the book *"Al-Ihsaan fi taqreeb Saheeh"* by Ibn Balbaan

It is a difficult methodology without doubt, and it is a great shame that his book *"The description of Eemaan and its branches"* that he worked so hard to produce has been lost, and its location is no longer known, in fact, Al-Hafidh Ibn Hajar indicated in *"Al-Fath"* that he had never became acquainted with it.

IN SUMMARY: THE BRANCHES OF EEMAAN

Al-Hafidh, may Allâh have mercy upon him, wrote a summary of the branches of *Eemaan* from that which a number of the people of knowledge gathered together, so he produced a summary of the branches of *Eemaan* that was of great benefit. He (may Allâh have mercy upon him) said:

"I summarized the narrations of what I mentioned, and that was that the branches are divided into the actions of the heart, the actions of the tongue, and the actions of the body":

The actions of the heart: *are the beliefs and intentions and they consist of twenty four attributes: belief in Allâh, which includes belief in His physical self, His characteristics, His oneness because there is nothing like Him and everything other than him is created. Belief in His angels, His books, His messengers, and the divine decree: the good of it and the bad. Belief in the hereafter, which includes belief in the questions in the grave, the resurrection, the reckoning, the scales, the bridge, and heaven and hell. Love for Allâh, loving and hating for His sake, love for the*

94

Prophet, and belief of his ennoblement, which includes sending the prayers upon him, and following his Sunnah.

Sincerity, which includes leaving off of riyaa and nifaaq. Repentance, fear, hope, gratitude, trustworthiness, patience, satisfaction with the judgment, trust, mercy, and humility, which includes reverence of the elderly and mercy for the young; and leaving off arrogance, conceit, envy, spite, and anger.

Actions of the tongue: *consist of seven attributes: pronouncement of Tawheed, reciting the Quran, learning knowledge and teaching it, supplication and remembrance, which include seeking forgiveness and leaving off idle speech.*

Actions of the body: *consist of thirty eight attributes, fifteen of which are specific to the person, they are literal and religious purification, which includes keeping away from impurity. The obligatory and supererogatory prayers and likewise the Zakaat. Freeing a slave, and generosity, which includes feeding the poor; and honoring the guest. The obligatory and*

95

supererogatory fasts, Hajj and Umra, Tawaaf, Itikaaf, seeking the Night of Qadr, and fleeing for the religion, which includes hijrah from a country of shirk. Fulfilling oaths, contemplating Eemaan and performing expiations.

From these actions of the body: *are six attributes that are connected with relatives, and they are self-restraint by way of marriage, upholding the rights of the family, honoring the parents and not being ungrateful. Nurturing your children, keeping the ties of kinship, obeying the slave owner, and lenience with the slave.*

From these actions also: *are those that are connected with all people in general, and they are seventeen attributes: performing the act of leadership justly, sticking with the people of the Sunnah, obeying those placed in authority, and rectifying between the people, which includes fighting the Khawarij and the oppressors.*

Cooperation upon good: *which includes ordering the good and forbidding the evil. Enforcing capital punishment, and jihad, which includes al-marabitah (being prepared to face the enemy). Keeping the trust, which includes the*

96

*distribution of the khumas (one fifth of the spoils
of war that Allâh ordered to be given to the
needy), fulfillment of a loan, honoring the
neighbor, having good dealings, gathering wealth
from permissible sources, and spending wealth
responsibly, which includes leaving off of
squander and waste. Returning the salaams,
supplication for the one that sneezes, protecting
the people from harm, keeping away from
heedlessness, and removing the harm from the
path. These are sixty nine attributes, and it is
possible to count them as seventy nine with the
extra that was not included with those attributes
that were mentioned and Allâh knows best." [75]*

However it is necessary to know that limiting
these branches and counting them is not a
condition of *Eemaan*, rather it is enough for the
Muslim to read the Book of Allâh and the
Sunnah of His messenger ﷺ (may peace
and blessings be upon him); To perform the
command in them both (i.e. the book and the
Sunnah); and to refrain from those things that
have been forbidden in them both (i.e. the book
and Sunnah), and to believe all that we are

---

[75] In the book *"Fath-ul-Baari"* (1/52 and 53)

informed of in them. So whoever does that then they have performed the branches of *Eemaan*. The servants' portion of these branches depends on his portion of knowledge, action, and application of the Quran and *Sunnah*.

This is why Qadi Iyyad (may Allâh have mercy upon him) said:

"A group took it upon themselves to restrict the branches by way of Ijtihaad. The ruling in that regard I was difficult to attain. And there's no harm in not knowing the limit of that in detail in regards to Eemaan." [76]

If the resemblance of the believer is like that of the date tree and the resemblance between them is apparent in many ways, some of which were indicated in that which has preceded, then verily the believers in their homes are like many date trees in a blessed garden; they produce the best of fruit and nourishment all the time by permission of their Lord.

---

[76] In the book *"Fath-ul-Baari"* (1/52)

Moreover, if this is the resemblance of the believers in their homes then the rectifiers amongst them are like the gardener in his garden. It is well known that not all gardeners are on the same level of efficiency, ability, and good cultivation of the date trees, vegetation, and fruits, rather they differ considerably, of which Allâh is All-knowing; And there is no harm here in making three examples of three kinds of gardeners or cultivators in their farms to make clear the meaning and intent.

THREE EXAMPLES OF GARDENERS

The 1st Example:

A gardener, whose description, as the onlooker can see, is not happy. He has a harsh disposition, is red eyed, hot tempered, controlling, and impatient. He treats the date trees in his garden in a strange manner: leaving off the correct gardening methods and renouncing the correct way. He does this as he believes that his date trees are not deserving of the term *"date tree"* and he refuses to provide them with the proper cultivation and care unless they are correct, sound, complete and without deficiency in any way. So if, he finds a deficiency in one of his trees, or a sickness, or a defect inside of it, then he will begin to remove it from its foundations, rip its roots out and then throw it as far away as possible behind these walls of his garden. This is his way with his date trees: he does not place any importance on rectification and he does not take care of their cultivation or care. There is no doubt that the inevitable result of this action is the wasting of his garden, the trees coming apart, and the dwindling of the garden bit by bit.

100

The 2nd Example:

Another gardener who deals with his date trees
in a strange and bizarre way. He believes that it
is not correct to describe the tree as deficient in
any way. Just as, the dead date tree is not
benefitted at all by the presence of its parts then
so too in life, it is not harmed by the presence of
a defect in some of its parts. So in his opinion,
all the date trees are of the same standard, the
sick tree, the one that has a defect, and the one
that is healthy and correct. In fact, he declares
them to be all equal like the teeth of a comb, no
difference between them, no distinction and no
preference for one over another. He even gives
orders not to differentiate between the fruit of
the date trees and the types of dates from that
which is known by necessity by everyone to
make a distinction and preference in this regard.

This strange precept brings forth in the gardener
a strange way to deal with his garden. He is not
consistent with his cultivation of the garden; he
does not place importance in its irrigation; he
does not take care of it, and he does not pay

attention to it. Many of his date trees could become sick, or a number of them could be afflicted by some type of defect or disorder or ruin and yet he does not care or take notice. In fact with all of that he still believes in their integrity, completeness and soundness. There is no doubt that the inevitable result of this behaviour will be the loss of his garden and its fast demise.

The 3ʳᵈ Example:

A gardener brought up on gardening and cultivation since his youth. He is wise in his care for his garden and knowledgeable in the ways of attending to it and the things that bring about their strength and growth. He is patient upon the harshness of it and the difficult living. He is efficient in performing the necessities and requirements of the date trees, and he gives them the utmost care from when they are first sowed. He is diligent with the watering, rectification, and removal of weeds that could hurt and harm the trees. He cares for all of his trees without any differentiation between the strong, the weak, the good and the bad. Those of the trees that are strong, correct, and without defect are a delight to his eyes; and he is pleased by their goodness, their quality, and their completeness. He continues to work with them to create the causes for their firmness and endurance.

Those that are weak, sick, or are deficient in growth make his heart hurt and sad for their weakness and deficiency. He deals with them discerningly. He does not rip them out by the roots and throw them out of the garden, and he does not neglect them altogether, leaving them without any cultivation or care. Rather he uses, for the sake of their rectification and improvement, discerning measures, sound methods, and correct, orthodox ways which are all concerned with the rectification of his date trees, giving them strength and good growth, and he always consults the people of merit, understanding and experience. But before all of this he has a strong connection with Allâh and has absolute trust in Him. He disassociates himself from any ability or power knowing that he has no might and no strength except with Allâh the Almighty by whose hand are the reigns of control. Due to this he keeps his tongue moist with the remembrance of Allâh and frequently repeats the saying *"Maa shaa Allâh la hawla wa la quwwata illa billaha"* (Whatever Allâh wills, there is no might and no power except with Allâh).

His garden never ceases to grow, and his date trees are always plenty and never cease to increase in beauty. They produce fruits of many types and the best of nourishment all the time by permission of his Lord.

As well as this he is great in his praise for his Lord, plenty in his commendation of Him, knowledgeable that the grace is by the hand of Allâh, He gives it to whom He wills, and Allâh is the possessor of great beneficence.

These are three examples that make clear the types of people that busy themselves with rectification and a clarification of their different methods. There's no harm in clarifying an affair that is not hidden from the reflective person, and that is that the **first example:** is that of the Mu'tazilah and the Khawarij in their dealings with the servants of Ar-Rahman, the believers. They are the people of harshness, roughness and vitriol. From their corrupt beliefs is the ruling that the one who commits a major sin exits from *Eemaan* and on the Day of Judgment he will be entered into the hellfire for eternity.

The second example: is that of the Murjiah and the way they deal with the believers. They are the people of apathy, idleness, and indifference to the affairs of the believers. This arose from the fatalism of their beliefs as they view actions as not being a part of *Eemaan*. They differ greatly in this belief to the extent that some of them have even come to be of the opinion that *Eemaan* is not harmed by sin, no matter how great, just as disbelief is not benefitted by obedience.

The third example: is that of *Ahlus Sunnah wal Jama'ah*. The people of the truth and *isitiqama* (uprightness). The people of the just and moderate methodology. The best of mankind, the most balanced in character. Those that rise above the shortcomings of the neglectful and do not reach the extremes of the extremists.

Ahlus Sunnah's standpoint in regards to the sinners among the Muslims is that they do not declare them to be disbelievers or take them out of the religion like the Khawarij and the Mu'tazilah. They also do not judge them to have complete and perfect *Eemaan*; rather they say:

"They are believers with deficient Eemaan"

So they love them for that which they possess from *Eemaan*, and they hate them for that which they possess from sin. They are merciful with them; they advise them; they are diligent upon their rectification and guidance, using the mildest of approaches, with the best character, and within the limits of the *Shariah* and its known foundations.

And with this the treatise has been completed, and Allâh knows best. May Allâh's Salaah and Salaam be upon our prophet Muhammad, his family and all of his companions.[77]

---

[77] It (the treatise) regarding the original was a lecture that was given at the Islamic University of Medina in 1417AH. (in correspondence to 1996) Afterwards it revisions were completed and some additions were made to it; and by way of Allâh alone success is granted.

Made in the USA
Columbia, SC
30 April 2024